SOCIAL PSYCHOLOGY: AN EXPERIMENTAL APPROACH

Meredith W. Watts

BASIC CONCEPTS IN PSYCHOLOGY SERIES
developed at The University of Michigan
Edward L. Walker, Editor

GENERAL

PSYCHOLOGY AS NATURAL AND SOCIAL SCIENCE	Edward L. Walker
TEACHING THE BEGINNING COURSE IN PSYCHOLOGY	Edward L. Walker and Wilbert J. McKeachie
A LABORATORY MANUAL FOR THE CONTROL AND ANALYSIS OF BEHAVIOR	Harlan L. Lane and Daryl Bem
QUANTIFICATION IN PSYCHOLOGY	William L. Hays
BASIC STATISTICS	William L. Hays

PSYCHOLOGY: A NATURAL SCIENCE

NEUROPSYCHOLOGY: THE STUDY OF BRAIN AND BEHAVIOR	Charles M. Butter
SENSORY PROCESSES	Mathew Alpern, Merle Lawrence, and David Wolsk
PERCEPTION	Daniel J. Weintraub and Edward L. Walker
HUMAN PERFORMANCE	Paul M. Fitts and Michael I. Posner
CONDITIONING AND INSTRUMENTAL LEARNING	Edward L. Walker

PSYCHOLOGY: A SOCIAL SCIENCE

MOTIVATION: A STUDY OF ACTION	David Birch and Joseph Veroff
THE CONCEPT OF HUMAN DEVELOPMENT	Elton B. McNeil
PSYCHODYNAMICS: THE SCIENCE OF UNCONSCIOUS MENTAL FORCES	Gerald S. Blum
ASSESSMENT OF HUMAN CHARACTERISTICS	E. Lowell Kelly
COGNITIVE PROCESSES	Melvin Manis
SOCIAL PSYCHOLOGY: AN EXPERIMENTAL APPROACH	Robert B. Zajonc

SOCIAL PSYCHOLOGY: AN EXPERIMENTAL APPROACH

ROBERT B. ZAJONC

The University of Michigan

WADSWORTH PUBLISHING COMPANY, INC., BELMONT, CALIFORNIA

To Donna, Peter, Michael, and Joseph

L. C. Cat. Card No.: 66–12645

Printed in the United States of America

SERIES FOREWORD

Basic Concepts in Psychology was conceived as a series of brief paperback volumes constituting a beginning textbook in psychology. Several unique advantages arise from publishing individual chapters as separate volumes rather than under a single cover. Each book or chapter can be written by an author identified with the subject matter of the area. New chapters can be added, individual chapters can be revised independently, and, possibly, competitive chapters can be provided for controversial areas. Finally, to a degree, an instructor of the beginning course in psychology can choose a particular set of chapters to meet the needs of his students.

Probably the most important impetus for the series came from the fact that a suitable textbook did not exist for the beginning courses in psychology at the University of Michigan—Psychology 100 (Psychology as a Natural Science) and Psychology 101 (Psychology as a Social Science). In addition, no laboratory manual treated both the natural science and social science problems encountered in the first laboratory course, Psychology 110.

For practical rather than ideological reasons, the initial complement of authors comes from the staff of the University of Michigan. Coordination among geographically dispersed authors seems needlessly difficult, and the diversity of points of view in the Department of Psychology at Michigan makes the danger of parochialism quite small.

Each author in the Basic Concepts in Psychology Series has considerable freedom. He has been charged to devote approximately half of his resources to elementary concepts and half to topics of special interest and emphasis. In this way, each volume will reflect the personality and viewpoint of the author while presenting the subject matter usually found in a chapter of an elementary textbook.

INTRODUCTION

There are in all disciplines unsolved problems that for years remain forgotten and ignored. Formerly important, they lie aside, swept by surging waves of new interests. Eventually, some of them find their way back to the laboratories. But many remain in obscurity, even though they also could profitably avail themselves of new methods and new ideas. In social psychology, modern theoretical and experimental trends have overshadowed many problems once in the very forefront of the field.

This book attempts to focus attention on neglected, unsolved problems of social psychology. Some material here has been resurrected from the past, and some has been reclaimed from zoology. The remainder of the material deals with current interests but does not always follow the beaten paths. This short text may not give the most faithful representation of today's main interests in social psychology, but no text can be *fully* representative of current research trends. To present a full picture of the current field of social psychology, instructors may want to supplement this text with lectures and with assignments from other modern texts of their choice.

No book is a product of one man alone, and I am indebted to many colleagues who gave freely of their time, advice, and criticism. In particular, my warm thanks go to Daniel Katz, Eugene Burnstein, Nickolas B. Cottrell, J. Allan Winter, Melvin Manis, and Gerald S. Blum.

CONTENTS

THE DEVELOPMENT OF SOCIAL PSYCHOLOGY

1

WHAT IS SOCIAL PSYCHOLOGY?

Scientific disciplines do not have sharp and stable boundaries. Areas of scientific endeavor very often overlap. The interests and problems of all fields continually change. Consequently, a definition of social psychology, like the definition of any other science, will at best *point* to the scope and to the more permanent interests in the field. The following is such a definition.

The various fields of psychology are all concerned with the analysis of behavior. If he is interested in *learning*, the psychologist studies behavior as it is influenced by past practice and by its reinforcement history. If he is interested in *perception*, the psychologist analyzes responses as they are modified by changes in physical stimuli. If he is interested in *motivation*, he analyzes responses in terms of the antecedent states of deprivation or arousal. All these psychologists would be classified in different fields, but not because they study different behaviors. On the contrary, they all may study an identical set of responses. What distinguishes these psychologists is that they analyze responses in terms of different antecedents. For instance, the rat's response of "turning left in a T-maze" may be analyzed in terms of the number of reinforced trials that have been given to the animal (the psychology of learning); or in terms of the level of the animal's hunger (the psychology of motivation); or in terms of the physical properties of the right arm of the maze as opposed to those of the left arm (the psychology of perception). If all of the above variations—reinforcement, deprivation, and physical stimulation—are held constant, and if we observe the rat's responses of "turning left in the T-maze" when there happens to be one other rat in the right arm of the maze, we become social psychologists.

Social psychology deals with *behavioral dependence and interdependence among individuals*. By "behavioral dependence" we mean a relation among the behavior of a number of individuals, such that a given behavior of one or more individuals is a cause or an occasion for change in the behavior of one or more other individuals. "Interdependence" simply means that the dependence is mutual and reciprocal. Note that the behaviors involved need not occur at the same time. The behavior under the influence of others need not *immediately* follow the

I

behavior causing or precipitating it. The social psychologist may study the way in which the responses of a given individual become coordinated to the behavior of another individual when both engage in a joint task, or he may study the degree to which a particular behavior pattern depends on the sort of up-bringing the subject received—that is, how his parents, teachers, and peers behaved long in the past. Social psychology, then, asks questions about the behavioral relations of individual to individual in general, but primarily of man to man, and occasionally of animal to animal.

Social psychology is not a "kind" or a "school" of psychology. It is definitely a *branch* of psychology, and it takes full cognizance of the laws of general and experimental psychology. Its language is commensurate with the language of other fields of psychology, and its laws consistent with the laws of general psychology.

THE DEVELOPMENT OF SOCIAL PSYCHOLOGY

Around 250 B.c. the Greek astronomer Eratosthenes calculated the circumference of the earth by comparing the angles of the noon sun in Alexandria and in Aswan, which lies directly to the south on the tropic of Cancer, and where on the day of the summer solstice the angle of the noon sun is exactly 90°. His results—among the first scientific observations recorded in history—differ from the present estimates by about 180 miles, or less than 1 percent.

The velocity of light was first measured in 1675 by the Danish astronomer Ole Römer, who compared the observed eclipses of Jupiter's moons with predictions based on precise theoretical calculations. His results also agree very closely with the present ones.

The speed with which the nervous impulse is propagated was first accurately measured in 1850 by the German physicist Helmholtz. He obtained measurements by comparing delays in the muscular responses in the leg of a frog for nerves of different lengths.

The first experimental observation in social psychology was performed in 1897 by Triplett. It dealt with the effects of competition on human performance. Triplett measured the average time required to execute 150 winds on a fishing reel. His subjects performed the task while working alone and while competing in pairs against each other. Performance was found to improve when carried out in competition.

The first scientific measurement preceded the first social-psychological measurement by twenty-one centuries. Social psychology, then, is almost entirely the product of this century and of this generation. Social psychologists credited with the crucial developments in the field are still alive. The author of the first social-psychological text, William McDougall, died only in 1938. More than 90 percent of all social-psychological research has been carried out during the last twenty years, and most of it during the last ten.

Why did social psychology fail to develop earlier?

Was the rise of social psychology inhibited by the lack of special technology? The measurements performed by Eratosthenes, Römer, and Helmholtz all required some previous knowledge and employed techniques developed earlier. Eratosthenes needed geometry, which Euclid systematized in about 300 B.C. Römer's findings could not have been possible without the telescope. The instrument he used was constructed by Father Scheiner in 1630. It contained two convex lenses and was a direct improvement of the prototype invented by Galileo in 1609. Helmholtz could not have made his observations without the work of Galvani, who was first to note the electrical properties of neural transmission in 1790 and who discovered a method of electrically stimulating a leg severed from a frog's body. In each of these examples the necessary antecedent knowledge or technique preceded the final measurement by about fifty years.

But the knowledge and technique necessary for Triplett's experiment were available at least 4,000 years ago. All he needed was (a) people who, under observation, would work alone and in groups; (b) a task that they could perform under both conditions; and (c) a means of counting units of work on this task per unit of time. Since these prerequisites were certainly present in the Egypt of the pharaohs, some other factor must explain why the development of social psychology was arrested for centuries.

Consider two alternatives. First: Social-psychological experiments were not attempted earlier because social-psychological questions were not asked until the twentieth century. Second: Social-psychological questions were asked before, but for one reason or another they were not answered before the twentieth century.

Let us first consider the former, for it can be easily rejected. Questions about human interdependence must have been asked as soon as there was the dimmest realization that men *are* interdependent. Those who built empires and those who built pyramids, coordinating the efforts of hundreds of thousands of men, must have encountered innumerable problems of human interrelationships and must have, therefore, raised some social-psychological questions. Ancient law shows clear examples of concern with these problems. Hammurabi's Code and the Old Testament attempted to regulate interpersonal relationships that were sources of problems for society. Seven of the Ten Commandments address themselves quite explicitly to the regulation of interpersonal conduct.

The social-psychological questions asked in the past were, to be sure, either about the moral nature of human interdependence, or about the control and manipulation of human behavior. (Machiavelli's *Il Principe* is a splendid example of this latter interest.) Neither type of question is strictly scientific. Those of the first type are ethical; those of the second are administrative and practical. Neither type is a direct concern of social psychology, but in order to ask an ethical or moral question, some social-psychological knowledge is necessary. In analyzing the ethics of human interdependence—such as those of slavery, of incest, or of property rights—one must invariably turn toward the analysis of its *consequences*. Do these consequences, for instance, violate some religious dogma or are they consonant with some moral precepts? Or, are the consequences of human interrelationships useful or harmful to society or to the parties involved? On the other hand, questions about the control of human interdependence require the knowledge of *antecedents*, for if one is interested in producing certain effects it is always useful and often necessary to know their causes. When man asked questions about antecedents and consequences, about causes and effects, he asked *scientific* questions.

Since man was already capable of asking scientific questions, the delay in the development of social psychology becomes even more curious. But there is a possible explanation. Men may have been satisfied that they already possessed answers to social-psychological questions. In all societies there are institutional mechanisms for regulating social behavior: law, custom, religion, and etiquette. In a way these mechanisms enable the members of the given society to *explain* and to *predict* social behavior. Because of their regulatory nature, these institutional mechanisms in themselves constitute antecedents of human relationships, for to regulate is in large part to determine. In all societies such mechanisms are explicitly identified, and they provide, therefore, a ready means for the explanation of social behavior. The policeman who, after giving you a speeding ticket, declares, "I hate to do it, Mac, but it's my job," provides you not only with an apology but also with an explanation of his behavior toward you. We have been satisfied with similar explanations for centuries.

The institutional mechanisms that regulate social behavior have also another important feature in common: they produce uniformity among the members of the given society. And because they lead to uniformity of social behavior, they facilitate its prediction. By definition, uniform events are more easily predictable than heterogeneous events. It is a reasonably safe prediction that you will drive about 35 mph when the posted speed limit is 35 mph.

To the extent that law, custom, religion, and etiquette provide satisfying explanations of social behavior and enable us to predict fairly reliably, social psychology cannot contribute a great deal more. But law, religion, custom, and etiquette have ceased to supply satisfying explanations. With the growth of civilization, man's life is regulated by these institutional mechanisms considerably less than it once was.

The Reformation introduced heterogeneity into spheres of behavior and belief governed by religious dogma. It also weakened the authority and influence of the church. Today's churches have only a fraction of the control they had in the days of the Inquisition. On the ashes of the feudal system, and in the wake of the bourgeois and industrial revolutions came freedom from institutional control in many areas of social behavior. The power of a modern employer over his workers can hardly be compared with the power of the feudal lord over his vassals. Threat and force were replaced by persuasion and advertising. Social behavior became more difficult to explain and to predict. Eventually man began to search for new explanations and for new ways of predicting events in the area of human interdependence. Social psychology is one of the developments of that search.

PLAN OF THIS BOOK

We define social psychology as the study of behavioral dependence and interdependence among individuals. Guided by this definition we shall try to introduce the reader to social psychology in terms of three major foci of analysis. The first section of the book deals with behavioral dependence; that is, the behavior of a single individual as it is influenced by others—or *social behavior*. The second section is concerned with the mutual and reciprocal behavioral dependence among individuals—or *social interaction*. The third and last section focuses attention upon the consequences of social behavior and interaction: social uniformity, group structure, and group performance—in short, it deals with *group processes*.

In each section the main problem areas and findings will be highlighted. In each case, a few experiments typical of those in the problem area under discussion will be presented to acquaint the student with the basic concepts employed in the theoretical analysis of these problems, and to illustrate the methods and techniques for dealing with the problems experimentally. These few "typical" experiments will be thoroughly discussed and their results examined in the hope that within at least one limited sector of the given problem area the student will gain a somewhat deeper and more intimate understanding than a catalog of "facts" usually provides.

Necessarily, then, many important and productive areas of social psychology will be left out. Among topics not treated here, or treated only in passing, are attitudes, attitude change, persuasion, socialization, the self, role relations, group cohesiveness, and leadership. They will be excluded so that we can go deeply into a few important sectors rather than superficially scan the whole field. Also excluded are problems that involve psychological processes operating primarily within a single individual—such as affiliation, aggression, and cognitive dissonance. Finally, because our introduction to social psychology is organized in terms of experimental paradigms, it is more apt to consider problems generated by exprimental results and by theory than by social ills. For this reason, chapters on juvenile delinquency, war, race relations, prejudice, industrial conflict, etc.—which can be found in many social-psychological texts—will not be found in this one. The student who wishes to become acquainted with the topics not treated here should consult his instructor for appropriate references.

PART ONE

SOCIAL
BEHAVIOR

Many clichés undeservedly substitute for understanding. One such cliché holds that man is a social animal. The accent in this cliché is on "social," and imbedded in it are a host of mistaken implications. Calling him a *"social* animal" seemingly resolves many questions about man and about so-called *"human* nature." It has been used to explain why people live in communities, why they form groups, organizations, and societies. The implication is that because man is "social" he will behave in certain "social" ways. "Social" has been stretched to cover a variety of different, and sometimes opposite, behaviors, to explain why there is polygamy and why monogamy; why there is loyalty to the group and why treason; why there is crime and why obedience to laws; why there is marriage and why divorce; why there is altruism and why egoism.

When the accent in the cliché is shifted to "animal," then the word "social" begins to acquire innate and instinctive qualities. For instance, in *The Descent of Man,* Darwin wrote:

> As man is a social animal, it is almost certain that he would *inherit* a tendency to be faithful to his comrades, and obedient to the leader of his tribe; for these qualities are common to most social animals. He would from an *inherited* tendency be willing to defend, in concert with others, his fellow-men; and be ready to aid them in any way, which did not too greatly interfere with his own welfare or his own strong desires.[1]

In all probability Darwin was wrong about the *inherited* nature of these tendencies. In 1810, more than 60 years before Darwin published *The Descent of Man,* a not too well-known French philosopher, Helvetius, expressed himself on this point with a remarkable clarity:

> Do men seek to make dupes? They exaggerate the force of sentiment and friendship, they represent sociability as an *innate affection* or principle. Can they in reality forget that there is but one principle of this kind, which is corporeal sensibility? It is to this principle alone, that we owe our self-love, and the powerful love of independence: if men were, as it is

---

[1] Italics mine.

said, drawn toward each other by a strong and mutual attraction, would the heavenly Legislator have commanded them to love each other, and to honor their parents? The command to love our fathers and mothers, proves that the love of our parents is more the effect of habit and education, than of nature. Would he not have left this point to nature, which, without the aid of any law, obliges men to eat and drink when they are hungry and thirsty, to open their eyes to the light, and keep their hands out of fire?

Again, calling man a "social animal" probably does not even distinguish him from other animals. Professor Wynne-Edwards of Aberdeen University expressed himself quite succinctly on this point (1962):

There seems to be no question of dividing the animal kingdom neatly into two camps, the one containing animals that are social and the other those that are not: rather it emerges, as might have been expected, that socialization is a general phenomenon, which from comparatively lowly and obscure beginnings has undergone progressive evolution, so that in the more advanced groups it has tended to become increasingly more conspicuous and complex. Although the extent to which social adaptations have been evolved in different animals, therefore, varies between wide extremes, the series is nevertheless a continuous one: the barnacle larva which at metamorphosis fixes itself or is inhibited from doing so, depending on the presence and number of other barnacle larvae already attached, is responding socially in a way that is not effectively different in principle from the one which animates the communal behavior of the social insects or the most highly socialized birds and mammals. In each case the behavior of the individual is conditioned by the presence and actions of other members of the population . . . (p. 127).[2]

As early as 1878 the French natural scientist and philosopher Espinas claimed that sociability is not "a restricted accidental condition found only among such privileged species as bees, ants, beavers, and men, but is in fact universal."

It is unfortunate that the field being introduced to the reader bears a "social" label—which, because it means so many different things, actually means very little. But even if the label "social" *explains* nothing specifically about man, it is still necessary for us to agree on what it *denotes,* for we shall have to use the word repeatedly. Since we define social psychology as the study of behavioral dependence and interdependence among individuals, "social" will mean a property of one organism's behavior which makes the organism vulnerable to behavior of another organism. In Part I, analysis will focus on the behavior of a single individual as influenced by other individuals. The influence exercised by those others can take several forms. The forms of influence

2 Wynne-Edwards, 1962; reprinted with permission of author and publisher.

selected for review in Part I correspond to the most common experimental situations employed in social-psychological research. We shall begin in Chapter 2 with the simplest case: the responses that a single individual emits in the presence of others; specifically, we shall examine changes in individual behavior produced by the presence of passive "spectators." In Chapter 3 we shall look into the question of what happens to the behavior of a single individual when it occurs in the presence of others engaged in the same activity. In Chapter 4 we will be concerned with how an individual benefits from the experience of others. Finally, in Chapter 5, we shall review the processes of social reinforcement—again paying particular attention to an individual's behavior that is under the control of social rewards or punishments.

In all chapters of Part I, analysis will focus upon the behavior of a single individual, taking into account the behavior of others as an antecedent condition. The four topics differ only in the complexity of this antecedent condition.

SOME CONFLICTING EXPERIMENTAL FINDINGS

Around the turn of the century, work on muscular effort, exertion, and fatigue was quite popular. Commonly this research was conducted by means of a curious instrument called the *ergograph*. There are various types of ergographs, depending on what particular muscles are being examined. A finger ergograph, for instance, is an apparatus consisting of a plate to which we strap the individual's arm, a weight suspended from the subject's finger, a metronome, and a recording device. Each time the metronome ticks, the subject must pull the weight as hard as he can. The distance that the weight travels is accurately recorded.

A German experimenter, Meumann, who was engaged in this sort of research in the early 1900s, had his students spend long evening hours working with the ergograph as experimental subjects. One evening Meumann unexpectedly came into his laboratory and found one of his students fully absorbed in his assignment. The subject's previous record over a period of several days had been quite uniform. Every evening the weight had traveled very nearly the same distance. However, as soon as Meumann entered the laboratory, the subject's output markedly and suddenly increased. Meumann, immediately noticing the change, discovered that output had increased without an apparent increase in exertion. This increase in muscular output was of particular significance because in ergographic work the individual is presumed to be always working at the upper limit of his capacity. Meumann's accidental observations led him to conduct further experiments, where similar effects deriving from the presence of others were essentially substantiated.

It may seem rather trivial to find that a student's effort increases under his professor's close scrutiny. But before we relegate Meumann's observation to the realm of the obvious, let us examine some related experimental data.

In 1925 Travis presented twenty-two college undergraduates with a revolving disc on which there was a small circular target. They were given flexible pointers with which to follow the rotating target as long as possible. The apparatus, called the pursuit rotor, was wired so that when the pointer was held on the target for one complete revolution, the subject obtained a score of 10. Scores were cumulated on special counters, and each student was given twenty training trials a day for several consecutive days. Each trial consisted of twenty revolutions, and since the disc revolved at 60 RPM, the duration of each trial was 20 seconds. The scores during the first few days were all around 150 per trial, but they began to rise—at first rapidly, then at a slower rate, and finally leveling off completely. When the subject reached a stable level, he was considered to have mastered the task, and training was concluded. The following day the subject was called to the laboratory and given five trials. After completing them, he was told that "a number of individuals wished to observe him follow the target." This "audience," consisting of from four to eight upperclassmen and graduate students, had been instructed to watch the subject quietly but attentively. Ten trials were administered to all subjects in the presence of this "audience."

In analyzing the results, Travis compared the subjects' performance while working in the presence of the audience with their prior performance in two ways. First, the average of the ten "audience" trials was compared with the highest ten consecutive scores that each subject received during training. The average of the highest ten consecutive "alone" scores was 172.26, while the average of *all* the "audience" trials was 177.42. Second, the highest score that each subject received during training was compared with the highest score he reached during his "audience" performance. The average of the former was 184.68 and of the latter 188.86. Both comparisons show that the subjects' performance in the presence of an audience surpassed their performance while working alone. But the differences between scores were not great.

In a more recent study, Bergum and Lehr (1963) obtained a similar increase in performance in a somewhat different setting and on a different task. The subject was placed in an isolation booth, where he found a panel outfitted with a circle of twenty red lamps. The lamps lit in sequence at a rate of 12 RPM. At times a light would fail to go on in its proper sequence. The lights were so arranged that during one hour of activity there were twenty-four failures. The subject's task was to depress a button whenever a light failed to go on normally. First, the subjects were given 20 minutes of training, and after a 10-minute rest they were asked to monitor the panel for a period of 2 hours and 15 minutes. Twenty subjects—all National Guard trainees—were "instructed to make themselves comfortable in the booths" and perform the task alone. The remaining twenty subjects—also National Guard trainees—were told that "from time to time a Lieutenant Colonel or a Master Sergeant would visit them in the booths to observe their performance." The visits occurred about four times during the testing. Bergum and Lehr divided the 135-minute testing period into five 27-minute intervals, and computed the average percentage of correct detections for each interval for both conditions of the experiment. Results, presented in Figure 1, show that

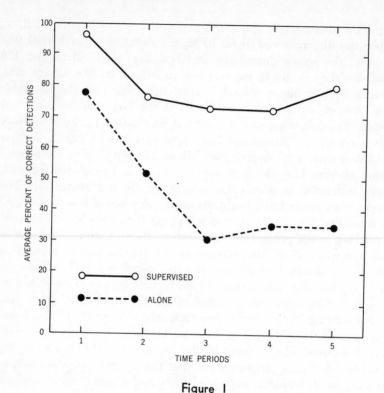

Figure 1

Accuracy on a monitoring task performed alone and under supervision. (From data by Bergum and Lehr, 1963.)

the superiors' visits resulted in superior accuracy. While the performance of both groups declined over time, due to fatigue, the detection accuracy of the supervised subjects remained on the average 34 percent higher than the accuracy of the trainees working alone, and during the last time-interval it was twice that of the subjects working alone.

The presence of passive spectators was also found to increase the speed of performance on such tasks as simple multiplication or serial word association (Dashiell, 1930). The effects of an audience we examined thus far seem to be generally beneficial, but let us look at another study. In 1933 Pessin had sixty subjects learn three lists of seven nonsense syllables. The subject learned one of the lists while he was alone, another while several spectators watched. (We shall ignore the third list here and compare only the "alone" and the "audience" conditions.) With the audience present, the subjects required an average of 11.27 repetitions for the learning of the seven-syllable list. When alone, they needed only 9.85

repetitions. The average number of errors made in the "alone" condition was 36.58, and in the "audience" condition 41.10. Similarly, Husband (1931), found that the presence of a spectator disturbed and interfered with the learning of a finger maze.

PRESENCE OF OTHERS AS SOURCE OF AROUSAL

Why do we sometimes seem to obtain an improvement in the presence of an audience and at times an impairment? In order to answer, we should examine some related results. Pessin did not collect data only on the *learning* of nonsense syllables; he collected similar data *after* the list had been fully learned. A few days following the learning of the task, the subjects were asked to recall the lists by relearning them alone and in the presence of spectators. Pessin used the so-called "saving score" to evaluate his results and to take into account the original differences in learning. Specifically, the scores were computed by the following formula:

$$100\left[1 - \frac{\text{Trials to relearn}}{\text{Trials to learn}}\right]$$

Pessin's results were quite clear, and now in agreement with those obtained by Travis and by Bergum and Lehr. The saving scores for the "audience" condition surpassed those in the "alone" condition. When subjects relearned the list in the presence of spectators, the average saving score was 49 percent. But relearning when alone resulted in a saving of only 38 percent.

Can we attribute the differences in audience effects to the differences in tasks? Can we say, for instance, that some tasks are facilitated and others impaired by the presence of spectators? This sort of generalization is certainly not justified, because in Pessin's experiment both effects were obtained for the same task.

Let us review the effects of an audience. (1) Travis used a pursuit-rotor task and found an improvement in performance in the presence of an audience. (2) According to Bergum and Lehr, the performance of a monitoring task improves when it is carried out under supervision. (3) Dashiell found that subjects complete simple tasks more rapidly in the presence of spectators. (4) Pessin found that nonsense-syllable learning is impaired, but that recall of the syllables is facilitated, in the presence of an audience.

There seems to be only one rather subtle consistency in these results. It appears that an audience impairs the acquisition of new responses and facilitates the emission of well-learned responses. The acquisition of new responses is called "learning," and the emission of previously learned responses is called "performance" (Walker, 1966; Fitts and Posner, 1966).

We can now simplify the generalization: *Learning is impaired and performance facilitated by the presence of an audience.* We must be careful, however, to note that the statement is tentative, because our evidence, although consistent up to now, is still very meager, and there may be conditions and tasks for which the statement is false. But, let's commit ourselves tentatively and see what happens.

Perhaps it would be fruitful to formulate our generalization in somewhat different terms to emphasize features of the problem thus far not considered. We recall that when learning nonsense syllables Pessin's subjects made considerably more errors in the presence of an audience than when alone. An "error" in verbal learning is simply a wrong response. The subject should have said DAC, for instance, but he said JIX. In many cases during the early stages of the learning process, a subject gives a greater number of wrong responses than right ones; the wrong responses are stronger and predominant. But once the individual has successfully learned the task, his behavior is dominated by correct responses. To formulate the original observation: *Audience enhances the emission of dominant responses.* If correct responses are dominant, the presence of an audience will increase the likelihood that correct responses occur; if wrong responses prevail, then the presence of an audience will enhance them.

If we can find a psychological process that enhances dominant responses and can be aroused by the presence of an audience, the conflicting experimental results on audience effects can be resolved. Such a psychological process indeed exists: *motivation.* Increased motivation increases the general arousal level of the organism; it activates it and energizes it (Birch and Veroff, 1966). The responses that the organism would normally emit in the given situation—the dominant responses—seem under increased motivation to be sharper, more intense, and quicker. This is well substantiated by Spence and his collaborators (for instance, 1956).

What remains to be determined is whether the presence of an audience increases the general arousal of the individual. The phenomenon of stage fright of actors and the nervousness of athletes engaged in public competition are effects easily observed and well known. They are accompanied by clear symptoms of arousal and activation—tension, alertness, and responsiveness. Some recent work has shown that the presence of others is closely associated with increased adrenocortical activity. This activity—as measured by the secretion of hydrocortisone, for instance—is a fairly reliable index of emotional arousal (Mason and Brady, 1964). It is a reasonable assumption, therefore, that the presence of others has motivational consequences (see Zajonc, 1965).

In this chapter, we have examined what seems to be the simplest kind of social effect—the effect deriving from the sheer presence of others. We found, first of all, that the sheer presence of others can markedly influence behavior in a generally consistent manner. But we found also that these effects are far from simple: audiences impair learning but facilitate performance.

At the same time we illustrated the intimate dependence of social psychology on general psychology. The tasks employed by the researchers in studying social effects were *standard psychological techniques:* the pursuit rotor, nonsense-syllable learning, and detection. To appreciate audience effects required distinguishing between two *standard psychological concepts,* learning and performance. The analysis also required that we search for a psychological process generated in the individual by the presence of an audience—a process that enhances the occurrence of dominant responses. The process assumed to play this role is *motivation,* another standard psychological concept. In chapters to come, the student will further see that other social effects require the systematic application of psychological concepts and psychological experimental techniques.

In the previous chapter we examined the simplest experimental paradigm of social-psychological research: the effects of the sheer passive presence of others on learning and performance. We shall now move toward a somewhat more complex paradigm. Again, we shall focus on individual behavior and what happens to it in the presence of others. But we shall now consider behavioral effects caused by *coactors*—that is, individuals engaged in the same activity.

F. H. Allport (1924), one of the important pioneer workers in social psychology, called a group of individuals engaged in the same activity the *coacting* group. Each person (or animal) in the group has his own task; each performs it at the same time and in the presence of others. The focus of observation, nevertheless, is still on the behavior of group members as individuals. This experimental paradigm, the oldest in social-psychological research, was the one Triplett used in 1897 to compare the speed with which individuals wound fishing reels when working alone and in groups.

Two types of coaction effects will be examined in this chapter. First, we shall be concerned with learning and performance in a coacting situation. Second, we shall describe coaction under stressful conditions; here we shall inquire into the effects of the presence of others, also in stress, on the tolerance of stress.

COACTION EFFECTS IN LEARNING AND PERFORMANCE

Another term introduced by F. H. Allport (1924) is *social facilitation*. This term implies that the *effects* of coaction are generally beneficial—that is, an individual's actions are enhanced by the presence of others doing the same thing.

We will begin our examination of coaction effects by looking at the behavior of infrahuman species for several reasons. First, these effects are relatively easy to isolate and to observe in animals. Second, results obtained with human subjects may tempt us to begin by looking into our own experience for explanations of behavior. Third, results from infrahumans will continue to remind us of the generality of the experimental paradigm of coaction.

One of the most dramatic social-facilitation effects was reported by Chen of the National Tsing Hua University of Peiping (1937). Chen's results, however, were obtained not on humans but on ants. Thirty-six ants were observed excavating nests while working alone, in groups of two, and in groups of three. On the first day each ant was placed by himself in a milk bottle filled half way with dry sandy soil, finely sifted. The ants were left there for six hours, and the time at which they began to build a nest was recorded. After this test the earth excavated by each insect was carefully weighed, to determine the amount of work accomplished. A few days later the same ants were placed in newly filled bottles, but now in groups of two. Again they remained in the bottles for six hours, and the same measurements were taken. Three days later they were observed in the same manner in groups of three. After all these tests, the insects were returned to newly filled bottles, but now again to work alone.

Table 1 shows Chen's results. The performance of these insects improves tremendously under the coacting conditions. The speed with which they begin building increases by a factor of about 6, and the

Table I

Solitary and coacting nest building by ants.
(From Chen, 1937.)

	FIRST TEST IN ISOLATION	GROUPS OF TWO	GROUPS OF THREE	SECOND TEST IN ISOLATION
Latency of nest building in minutes	192	28	33	160
Weight (per ant) in grams of earth excavated during a 6-hour period	232	765	728	182

amount of work performed by a factor of over 3. And there seem to be no aftereffects of the group experience, as we can see by comparing the first and the last columns of Table 1. One other finding that emerges is that the size of the group has in itself no additional effects: the presence of two other ants is not superior to the presence of only one other ant.

Is there any reason why we should not accommodate this finding under our previous generalization that the presence of others enhances dominant responses? Just because we are confronted with data on animal behavior, we need not assume that a different generalization applies. On the contrary, while human and animal behavior cannot always be equated, unless we have good *a priori* reasons to believe otherwise, it is best to act as if a generalization made about behavior applies universally to all species. If there are exceptions, the generalization will eventually be modified. It is unwise to complicate our analysis by agreeing at the outset that there are such exceptions.

To determine whether Chen's findings are consistent with our generalization we must know two things. First, given Chen's experimental conditions, is nest building a well-established dominant response of the ant? Second, does the presence of another coacting partner act to increase the general drive level of the ant? The answer to the first question is fairly obvious. Nest building is an instinctive skill and requires no learning. Put an ant near some soil, and within a short time it will build a nest, if it does not already have one in the vicinity. The second question is a matter of some conjecture. We noted in the previous chapter that there is strong evidence to show that the presence of others results in an increased general drive level of the organism. Recent studies extend this evidence to animal species (see Zajonc, 1965).

If coaction, like audience, increases the organism's general drive level, then it should enhance performance but inhibit learning. Gates and Allee (1933), also working with insects, compared maze learning in the cockroach when the training was given to these subjects alone, in pairs, and in groups of three. The maze consisted of a pan of water with three connected runways suspended over the surface. The runways were arranged in the shape of the letter "E." The goal of the maze was a dark bottle at the end of the middle runway where the cockroaches, which are photophobic insects, could escape from the noxious light.

In Figure 2 Gates and Allee's results are plotted in times required for successful runs over the first twenty-five trials. The coacting cockroaches learned considerably less efficiently than the solitary ones. On the first five trials the solitary cockroaches required an average of only about 5 minutes for a successful run, while the pairs needed 12 minutes, and groups of three almost 18 minutes.

Some birds, too, were found to learn less efficiently in pairs than alone. Klopfer (1958) reports that greenfinches learned to discriminate more rapidly between a palatable and unpalatable food source when working alone than when working in sexually unlike pairs. But was the reduced learning efficiency of these sexually unlike pairs due to increased drive level—or to a reduction in learning interest, brought about by the propitious pairing? Allee and Masure (1936), observed Australian parakeets learning to run a maze in pairs and alone. They, too, found a reduction in the speed of learning and an increase in the number of errors when the birds were paired. Moreover, regardless of whether two females, two males, or birds of opposite sex were paired, there always was a good deal of interference with learning, and the sexually unlike pairs showed no inferiority or superiority over the sexually alike pairs.

So far the results fit with our previous generalization. As a matter of

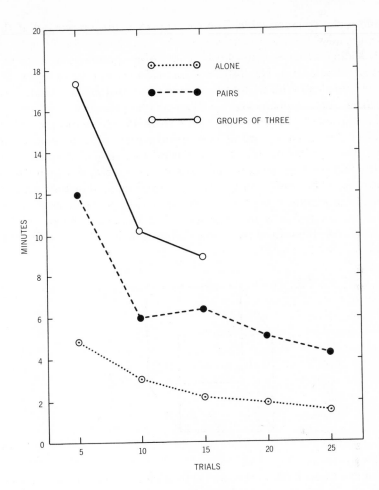

Figure 2

Maze learning in isolated and grouped cockroaches:
Average time per trial for the first day's test. (From
Gates and Allee, 1933, with permission of authors and
publisher.)

fact, the generalization may now be somewhat broadened: *Coaction, as*
well as audience, enhances performance and impairs learning.

All of the results so far in this chapter dealt with animals. Does
our generalization apply to human subjects? One of the best-known
experimental programs in human coaction was undertaken by F. H.
Allport in 1920. Allport on two occasions carefully administered various
types of tests to a large number of subjects. On one occasion the subjects
worked alone in separate cubicles, and on the other they worked together

sitting around a common table. Those in separate cubicles worked at the same time and were monitored by common time signals. In order to be sure of dealing with coaction effects alone, Allport attempted to reduce competitive tendencies. He instructed his subjects not to compare the results of their tests, and he told them that the research staff would also refrain from such comparisons.

Allport used six types of tasks: (1) A *chain-association task*, in which the subject was given a word at the top of a page with the instruction that he was to write beneath it a new word that immediately came to mind. His first response was then taken as the new word, to which a new association must be made—and so on for a fixed interval of time. (2) In the *vowel-cancelation task* the subject was asked to cross out all the vowels from a set of newspaper articles. (3) In one of the *reversible-perspective tasks* the subject was shown a line drawing of a cube, such as this one:

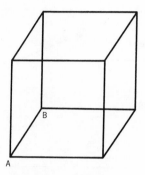

The cube can be seen "from the top" with A closer than B to the viewer, or "from the bottom" with B closer than A. The subject was asked to alternate rapidly his perception of the orientation of the cube. In another form of this test the objective was to prevent such reversals from occurring as long as possible. (4) In the fourth type of task, the subject was asked to perform *multiplications*. (5) In the *problem-solving task* the subject was asked to refute false syllogisms. (6) The *judgment task* consisted of rating pleasantness of odors and the magnitudes of several weights.

The results of Allport's experiments are often quoted to demonstrate the beneficial effects of working in groups as opposed to working in isolation. In all but the problem-solving and judgment tests, performance was at higher rates in a group than in isolation.

Why did problem solving suffer from coaction? Unlike serial association, multiplication, or vowel cancelation, false-syllogism analysis requires novel and often nonobvious solutions. As in Pessin's nonsense-syllable task (see Chapter 2, p. 12), the incorrect-response tendencies are quite strong. The subject is more likely to draw a wrong conclusion when there are many wrong ones—and just one correct. Again, if motivation increases the probability of the dominant responses, and if strong incorrect-response tendencies prevail, an increase in motivation can only be detrimental.

We have no data on whether coacting subjects performed better or worse on the judgment test. We do know that they made fewer extreme judgments. Unpleasant odors were rated less unpleasant, and pleasant ones less pleasant. Heavier weights were judged to be somewhat lighter and the lighter ones heavier. In general, then, under the coacting condition, judgments became more moderate and more uniform. Because these effects represent a different social-psychological problem, we shall leave Allport's findings about judgments until Part III (Chapter 8), where tendencies toward uniformity in groups will be discussed.

Let us now turn to an experiment that involves *learning* in the presence of others who are learning the same task. Imagine an aquarium with a vertical partition made of wire screen running the full width and depth of the tank. In the center of the partition is a conical opening, through which a fish can pass from one chamber to another. The opening is outfitted with a sliding metal gate. We now have a "maze" for fish. In 1934 Welty taught some common goldfish (*Carassius auratus*) to swim mazes of this type, rewarding them with a bit of a worm. On each trial the subjects were placed in the rear chamber of the tank, a red light was turned on in the front chamber, and the metal gate opened. As soon as a fish passed through the cone into the front chamber, it was fed a morsel of a "freshly cut earthworm impaled on the end of a feeding needle." On each trial Welty noted the time that elapsed between the turning on of the red light and the time at which the fish successfully passed through the conical opening. The fish were trained in this manner one at a time, in pairs, in groups of four, and in groups of eight. Four different experiments were conducted, each with some procedural detail slightly modified. In one the red light was made brighter, in another the fish were given a nine-day period of adaptation to the aquariums, and in the last the intertrial interval was changed. We have combined Welty's results from the four experiments and plotted them in Figure 3. Each point in the graph represents the average time interval between the onset of the red light and the subject's entry into the front chamber, computed for blocks of two consecutive trials. It is quite clear from the results that the coacting fish learned more rapidly than the isolated ones. Moreover, the larger the group, the stronger was the effect. The finding seems to contradict our previous generalization: Maze learning in fish

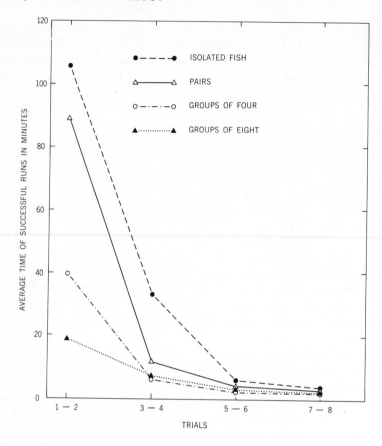

Figure 3

Maze learning in isolated and grouped goldfish. (Redrawn from data reported by Welty, 1934.)

appears to be facilitated by the presence of others also learning the maze.

But there is a clue to our puzzle. Welty carried out further experiments. When placed in the maze with a previously trained fish, an untrained fish learned considerably faster than when paired with another untrained fish. The sophisticated member of the pair seemed to act as a guide or a lure and to facilitate learning on the part of its untrained friend, which simply followed it around. As a matter of fact, Welty obtained the same results when an artificial metal fishing lure was substituted for the live "leader."

A similar effect was obtained in at least one experiment on human learning. In 1939 Gurnee studied subjects working alone and subjects working together in groups of from nine to fourteen individuals. Two tasks were used: (1) the learning of a so-called bolt-head maze; (2) the learning of a number maze. The bolt-head maze consists of a row of twenty pairs of bolts, each supplied with a metal pointer that can swing to one bolt or the other. The maze has a "signal" light, and the bolts are wired in such a way that the light will go on only if the pointer touches the "correct" bolt. For some pairs the left one and for others the right one is "correct." The subject's task is to learn how to light the signal for every pair of bolts. The number maze is similar, in that the subject is given twenty pairs of two-digit numbers and must learn to select the "correct" one for each pair.

The results of Gurnee's experiment were quite clear. On the bolt-head maze the "coacting" subjects made an average of only 5.21 errors, while the subjects working alone had 6.05. On the number maze, too, learning was better in the coacting condition than alone, the two error averages being 3.19 and 5.02, respectively.

As in Welty's experiment, the presence of other learners in Gurnee's study constituted not only a source of increased motivation but also a source of information. For the six first trials through the maze, the subjects made their choices aloud in addition to writing them down. In the coacting group they could hear each other quite well. After these six trials they were instructed to make their choices silently and in the same manner as in the "alone" condition. The average errors reported by Gurnee are errors alone for the seventh trial. Gurnee's explanation of the superiority of the group situation is as follows:

> But of probably greater importance were the suggestions to correct response which the group situation afforded. When acting collectively, a subject has, besides the ordinary cues to rightness or wrongness, the observable response tendencies of his fellows, and these may sometimes act to tip his judgment one way or the other. . . . Another factor of importance is the tendency of those who are correct in their choices to react more quickly than those who are wrong; so that doubtful members being, it is reasonable to suppose, most affected by the earliest suggestion, would be more often led to a right than to a wrong response.[1]

Thus, if most of the subjects *follow* the responses of the fastest learners, improvement in their learning rates must naturally be expected. The apparent contradiction between our generalization and these results seems to be reconciled. If the presence of others can provide the learner with cues for correct responses, then the harmful effects of the increased drive level might be diminished and even overcompensated for. We shall

[1] Gurnee, 1939; reprinted with permission of author and publisher.

consider the problem of how one organism can benefit by observing the responses of another in the chapter to follow. But let us first review another interesting social-facilitation effect.

SOCIAL SUPPORT

We have found thus far that performance of well-learned skills is generally facilitated by the presence of others, whether they be passive spectators or peers working on the same task. We have found that when individuals are able to *observe* one another, and when the behavior of others provides cues for correct responses, the rate of learning may be improved. This was equally true for Welty's fishes and for Gurnee's students. Let us now turn to a different sort of behavior. Can the presence of others help us endure pain? If we see others in stress, is our own stress easier to tolerate?

A group of psychologists working for the U.S. Army (Seidman et al., 1957) studied the ability of individuals to endure electric shock (a) when receiving the shock alone and (b) when in the presence of another also receiving it. The subjects, 133 enlisted men who had completed basic training, were measured for electric-shock tolerance in both conditions. In the "alone" condition, only the experimenter was present. In the coacting condition, another subject was brought in and ostensibly placed in the shock circuit. The enlisted men were told that their "partners would simultaneously receive a shock of exactly the same intensity," although the partners actually received no shock at all. In both conditions the subject himself, by means of a calibrated knob, increased the shock intensity to the maximum he could endure. The maximum shock tolerated by the individuals in the coacting condition was clearly greater. The authors concluded that "the perceived sharing of stress contributes importantly to stress tolerance."

It is probably important to a soldier, just past a successfully completed tour of basic training, to appear courageous to his comrades. How would rats react in this situation? Surely, they do not care about such vanities as valor and courage, and they have no country to defend or reputation to maintain. Shortly before the outbreak of World War II, Rasmussen (1939) performed the following experiment. Several albino rats, all litter mates, were deprived of water for 48 hours. They were then placed, alone or in groups of three, in a box that contained a dish of drinking water. The floor of the box consisted of a metal grill, wired to one terminal of an electric-shock circuit. A wire inserted into the water was connected to the other terminal.

After the thirsty rat was placed in the box, he would explore for awhile and soon find the water. He was allowed to drink with the circuit open for 5 seconds, and then the experimenter turned on a fairly strong current. From then on, the circuit remained closed, and each attempt to drink was accompanied by an electric shock.

The results were absolutely clear. The rats who were placed in the box in groups of three drank twice as often as the solitary rat. All, of course, endured shock when drinking. Courage?

Rasmussen presents another finding, which may lead us to a better understanding of the rats' behavior. He counted the number of times the rat approached the dish but immediately withdrew without drinking, over a period of 50 minutes in the box. On the average there were 26.4 such approach responses on the part of the coacting rats, and only 11.8 for the "alone" subjects. Figure 4 shows this behavior over the 50-minute period in the box. We see that the rate of approach to water is substantially higher for the coacting than for the solitary animals, and that it diminishes over time to approximately the same level.

The dominant response in this situation is "approaching the water dish." If the presence of others increases the general drive level of the organism, and therefore enhances the emission of dominant responses, then the coacting rats naturally would exhibit more approach behavior —that is, more attempts to drink. Like other dominant responses, drinking or eating increases in coaction (see Bruce, 1941). Katz (1937), for instance, placed together sated and hungry hens and found that ". . . in each case the first hen, which has already been fed, begins to eat again under the influence of the example set by the second, although she has already eaten to full satisfaction. An additional 60 per cent or more may be eaten under the social influence of the second hen." His results are thoroughly confirmed by experiments with other species—for example, rats (Harlow, 1932) and dogs (James, 1960).

The fact that in Rasmussen's experiment drinking also results in a painful shock need not discourage us from applying the motivational-enhancement principle, which has served us well thus far. Of course, the consequence of the shock is that the rats eventually reduce the frequency of their approach attempts, as Rasmussen's data indeed show. The "appropriate" response in this situation is to *avoid* the water dish, and it is this avoidance response which the rats must learn. But the tendency to drink increases in the presence of other animals, and an increase in this tendency is necessarily incompatible with avoiding the water dish. The fact that the grouped rats acquired this avoidance response more slowly than the solitary animals is entirely consistent with our generalization and with the results previously reviewed.

In yet another study Ader and Tatum (1963) confronted graduate and medical students with the following situation. The subjects, upon entering the laboratory in pairs and alone, were seated at a table and shock electrodes were attached to their legs. They were asked not to

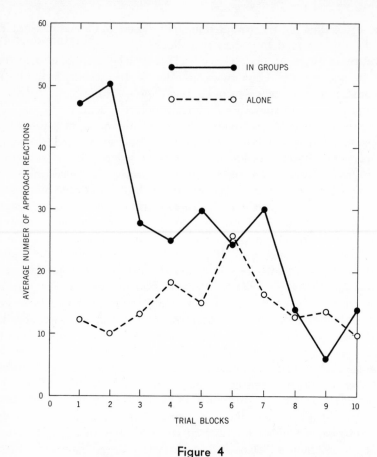

Figure 4

Approach behavior of solitary and grouped rats to a conflict-evoking stimulus. (Redrawn from data reported by Rasmussen, 1939.)

smoke, speak, get up from the chair, or touch the electrodes. The table, otherwise quite ordinary, was equipped with a red button. After placing the subject in position, the experimenter left the room without any further instructions. Now the individual would receive a shock for a period of ½ second every 10 seconds unless he pressed the red button. Pressing of the red button automatically delayed the shock for a period of 10 seconds. Note that the experimenter said nothing to his subjects about the purpose of the experiment, about the significance of the button, or about what they were expected to do.

In one condition the subjects worked alone; in another they were brought to the room in pairs and seated across from each other. The subject or the pair was considered to have learned the task if he (or they) did not receive more than five shocks in a period of 5 minutes. Ader and Tatum report that the individually conditioned subjects required, on the average, 11 minutes 35 seconds to reach this criterion of learning. Of the twelve pairs in Ader and Tatum's experiment, only two eventually learned the avoidance response. These two pairs required 46 minutes 40 seconds and 68 minutes 40 seconds to reach the criterion of learning.

Learning is thus impaired by the presence of others, regardless of whether it is the learning of approach or avoidance responses. But it is significant to note that after having learned how to avoid the shock, Ader and Tatum's subjects responded at considerably higher rates when in pairs than when alone. Thus, the performance of an avoidance response, once acquired, is enhanced in coaction.

In the study by Seidman and his colleagues, we must consider the task of the soldiers to be one requiring from them responses already learned—turning the dial to the right. Since "turning the dial to the right" was the dominant response, the presence of others simply enhanced its emission. Hence, "stress tolerance" may be a misleading label for the phenomenon that Seidman and his collaborators investigated. While the presence of others did effectively increase the intensity of the electric shock, we have no evidence about how well the enlisted men tolerated the pain caused by the shock.

We looked in this chapter at the behavior of an individual when he is with others doing the same thing. We found that the presence of others facilitates performance, probably by increasing the individual's general arousal level.

In general, the effects of coaction on learning, like the effects of audience, are negative. One principle of general psychology—motivation enhances the emission of dominant responses—helped us then to organize a variety of results on coaction, as well as on audience effects. Coacting groups of ants, cockroaches, goldfish, greenfinches, parakeets, albino rats, college sophomores, graduate and medical students, basic trainees, and National Guardsmen seem to follow the same set of psychological laws. These results would lead us to discourage "study groups" and other "togetherness" aids in learning, while they would simultaneously lead us to encourage taking exams in large groups and preferably in the presence of large audiences. This latter advice applies only when the student learned the material rather well. An audience during exams will otherwise have disastrous effects.

On the other hand, we also looked into two instances where learning was enhanced by the presence of other learners. The benefits of coaction in learning, however, obtain only if others provide the individual with *clues* about what is a correct and what is an incorrect response. We shall now consider other ways in which observing the experience of others can be beneficial.

LEARNING FROM EXPERIENCE OF OTHERS

4

E. R. Guthrie, a leading experimental psychologist, once said that the least ambiguous meaning of the word "mind" is the ability to profit from experience. One can kick a brick several times in succession, and the response of the brick each time will be passive. The response of a dog who is kicked several times—if one is successful in kicking him several times—is quite different. Not only will the dog, unlike the brick, resent the first kick; he will probably try to avoid the second, successfully avoid the third, and by the fourth kick begin avoiding on sight the individual dispensing kicks. What distinguishes a brick from a dog is that the latter can ". . . alter its response as a result of its past experience" (Guthrie, 1952). We can add to Guthrie's observation that creatures with "minds" can profit not only from their own experience but from the experience of others as well. (As a matter of fact, the more enterprising individuals can even reap benefits from the *in*experience of others. We will leave the concern over this latter phenomenon, however, to the criminologists.)

In the previous chapter, the results from Gurnee's experiments on the bolthead and the number maze, and from Welty's experiments on the aquarium maze could be explained only by assuming that the learners somehow benefited from each other's learning experiences. Let us now examine in closer detail the various processes that modify the responses of one individual when he is exposed to the learning experience of another. Three types of experimental situations will be considered: *imitation, vicarious learning,* and *conformity.*

IMITATION AND VICARIOUS LEARNING

One of the basic principles which for a long time seemed to explain the origin and maintenance of society, human and animal, was the "instinct of imitation." Until some twenty years ago, the innate nature of imitation was not seriously questioned. But in extensive studies on imitation with animal and human subjects, Miller and Dollard (1941) found no evidence of an innate propensity to imitate. In one of their experiments, for instance, several rats were first trained as "leaders" to make a simple T-maze discrimination. Other animals, one at a time, were then placed in the maze behind a leader, who had been trained to enter one or the other of its arms. On the very first trial, exactly 50 percent of responses were imitative. This is, of course, what one would expect purely by chance. If there were an instinct to imitate, Miller and Dollard claim, more than half the animals should have imitated.

Imitation exists when, for example, animal A responds and animal B immediately afterward makes the same response—and makes it consistently. If A turns left, B follows him and also turns left. If A turns right, B turns right. If this occurs consistently, B is presumed to imitate A. If B makes responses consistently opposed to those of A, he is said to counterimitate A.

Miller and Dollard found no particular difficulty in training children and rats to imitate and to counterimitate. If there were an instinctive tendency to imitate, they argued, it should have been more difficult to train counterimitation than imitation.

Miller and Dollard's conclusion about the acquired nature of imitation seems a bit too strong and a bit too general. Turner (1964) worked on imitation with 30-hour-old chicks. A silhouette of a hen was cut out of plywood. An axle was attached to the middle of the "hen's" body, enabling the experimenter to oscillate it as in pecking. Either a green or an orange grain was placed on the ground under its "beak." A wire mesh separated the baby chick from the "hen." The experimenter activated the mechanical hen, making it "peck" at a grain of particular color—for some chicks always green and for others always orange. He then presented both green and orange grains to the baby chicks. Out of the total of 349 pecks, the baby chicks made 228 (or 65 percent) at grains the same color as those the mechanical hen present was pecking. Turner's study seems therefore to suggest that a tendency to imitate might exist without prior learning as early as 30 hours after hatching. The following response of the duckling, too—which is a form of imitation occurring only at critical periods shortly after hatching—has been shown to be independent of previous learning (see Hess, 1962). A rapidly growing literature in the field of ethology continues to marshal convincing arguments that the role of instinctive and innate factors in the development of some forms of social behavior may have been seriously underestimated in past research (see Etkin, 1964).

When an animal or a child imitates or counterimitates, what has been learned? Do the "followers" merely learn to follow the "leader," or do they actually learn to respond to cues that control the leader's own behavior? Miller and Dollard were certainly able to teach rats to turn left (or right) when the leader rat did. Within fifty or sixty trials, an average rat learned to copy his leader nearly 100 percent of the time. And the leaders themselves turned left (or right) because a white card was placed at the end of the left (or right) arm of the maze, and because they were previously trained to find food near the white card. But in the process of learning to follow the leaders, did the followers also learn that the white card "meant food"? Did they, in short, only learn to copy their

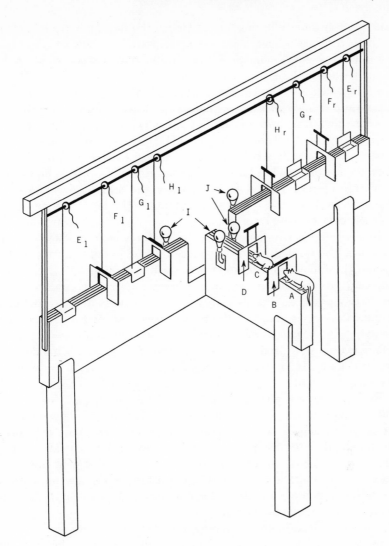

Figure 5

An elevated T-maze such as used by Church (1957).
A, follower's starting section; B, follower's starting
gate; C, leader's starting section; D, leader's starting
gate; E_l and E_r, leader's left and right water con-
tainers; F_l and F_r, leader's left and right goal gates;
G_l and G_r, follower's left and right water containers;
H_l and H_r, follower's left and right goal gates; I, left
cue lights; J, right cue lights. (Redrawn with per-
mission of author and publisher.)

leaders blindly and indiscriminately? Or did the followers, while learning to imitate, also learn how to behave appropriately in this situation once the leader was gone? Church (1957) attempted to answer this rather important question.

Church also used a T-maze, such as shown in Figure 5. First, six leaders were trained to run the maze. The leader-trainees, deprived of water for some time, were placed in the leader's starting section (C) on the short arm of the T-maze. A gate (D) immediately in front of the starting section was raised, and if the leader-trainee went into the arm designated as correct (left for some leaders, right for others), he found a thimbleful of water (E) at the far end of the arm. If he entered the wrong arm, he found no water in the thimble. The leaders were trained until their choices were errorless.

In the imitation training proper, all gates except the starting ones were open. The trained leader was placed in the leader's starting section (C) and the follower in the follower's starting section (A). Both gates (B and D) on the short arm of the maze were raised. The trained leader immediately proceeded to his correct arm, and the two outer goal gates (F_l and F_r) were lowered. If the subject followed his leader, the inner goal gate (H_l or H_r) closed behind him, and he found water in his thimble (G_l or G_r). If the subject went in the opposite direction, the inner goal gate (H_l or H_r) also closed behind him, but now he found no water.

Each subject was given ten trials a day, 3 minutes apart, for a period of fifteen days. Although they were allowed all the food they could eat, the rats were given access to water for only 90 minutes a day, and always immediately after the training session. The rats in this experiment, as in Miller and Dollard's, started on the first day of training at about the chance level of imitation (Figure 6). From the second day on, the rate of imitative responses increased, reaching nearly 100 percent at the completion of training on the fifteenth day.

After the fifteenth day of training, the animals were divided into two groups. In one group a cue light (I or J) would go on, on the same side the leader was turning. In the other group it would light on the opposite side. One hundred trials were given in these conditions. Then the followers were again placed in the maze for an additional twenty trials, with the leader now absent, and with the lights the only remaining cues. The experimenter's interest now was to determine whether the followers, in addition to having learned to follow the leader, had also learned to attend and to respond critically to the same cues that the leader was using.

The difference between the first 150 trials and the series of 100 trials with the cue lights represents the basic difference between what is known as *imitative learning* and *vicarious learning*. In imitative learning, the

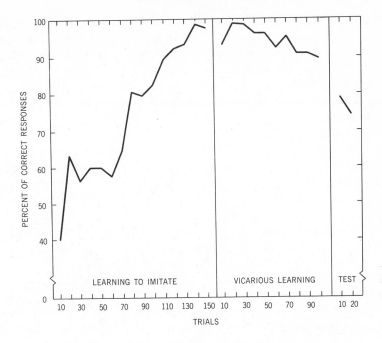

Figure 6

*Learning to imitate and vicarious learning of rats.
(Data reported by Church, 1957; redrawn with permission of author and publisher.)*

primary cues of the learner are the responses of the leader, while in
vicarious learning the cues that govern the leader's responses are available as cues to the learner as well.

It is plain from the graph that after the removal of leaders the animals were able to respond correctly to the lights alone. The average of
these responses was 77 percent. Since half of the rats had to select the
arm with the light on and half with the light off, the rats did not follow
or avoid the light itself. Evidently, the "leader" brought the learners'
attention to the relevant cues, thus accelerating the learning process.

Does the tendency to imitate (or to counterimitate), once learned,
generalize to situations other than those in which it has been acquired?
After they had taught rats to imitate in a T-maze, Miller and Dollard
(1941) transferred the rats to a completely different setup, consisting of
five elevated square platforms—one on each side of a central platform.
The platforms were separated by substantial gaps, over which the rats
could cross with some difficulty. The leader and the follower were placed
on the central platform, from which the leader would step across onto an-

other platform. Since there were four platforms to which the learner could turn from the central one, by chance alone a rat should have made the same response as his leader 25 percent of the time. In this situation, however, the animals previously trained to imitate now followed the leader 39 percent of the time, and those previously trained to go in the opposite direction followed only 18 percent of the time. In a similar manner, rats trained to imitate one leader followed another leader when the experimenter substituted one for the other.

Are imitation and vicarious learning limited to simple, uncomplicated responses? To find out, Warden (1936) designed a *duplicate-cage* method for observing vicarious problem solving of small primates and other small mammals. The method involves a cage with two identical compartments separated by a wire mesh. Each compartment contains the identical puzzle. An animal who has previously learned the puzzle—the leader—is placed in one of the compartments, and another animal who has no experience with the puzzle—the follower—is placed in the adjacent compartment. Both animals are restrained. A spotlight goes on in the leader's side, and he is released. Immediately, he begins to manipulate the puzzle, which requires him, for instance, to open a small door by moving two latches. Upon opening the door, the leader finds a raisin. This process—from spotlight to reinforcement—is repeated five times in rapid succession. Following the fifth "demonstration trial" the light goes off in the leader's compartment and on in the follower's. The follower is then released and allowed 60 seconds to solve his puzzle.

In one experiment with the duplicate-cage method Warden, Fjeld, and Koch (1940) used four different puzzles to study vicarious learning in monkeys: (1) pulling a chain that would raise a door; (2) opening a door by means of a hand knob; (3) opening a door by means of a latch; and (4) opening two latches and then opening a door. In each instance a raisin was behind the door for the animal. Each of six animals received six tests on each of the puzzles. In 110 of the 144 observations (4 puzzles $\times$ 6 tests $\times$ 6 animals) the naive followers solved the puzzles in less than 60 seconds, and in 57 of those 110 within less than 10 seconds. A naive monkey working alone takes considerably longer to solve puzzles of this sort—certainly longer than a minute.

Darby and Riopelle (1959), using rhesus monkeys, and Herbert and Harsh (1944), using cats, also demonstrated clear benefits of observational learning over direct learning. Herbert and Harsh also found that the learner derives a greater benefit from observing another cat's learning process than by observing the performance of a skilled cat. The leader's learning process displayed incorrect responses more frequently and clearly than did his skilled performance, and the follower cats benefited more from the observation of incorrect responses (wrong manipulations) than of correct ones. It appears that an animal may benefit from vicarious learning by eliminating, before the learning process begins, the many incorrect response tendencies with which he might otherwise approach the problem.

Is "observing" a *sufficient* condition for learning? Most learning theories hold that in order for an animal to acquire a given response tendency, the animal must repeatedly emit the response, and reinforcement must immediately follow. Are these conditions satisfied in vicarious learning?

Let us examine the results of a recent experiment in which learning was accomplished without any apparent reinforcement (Berger, 1962). In Berger's study a subject was called into a laboratory for an experiment with the announced purpose of measuring some physiological reactions to stimuli such as buzzers or lights. The measure actually taken was the Galvanic Skin Reaction (GSR), which is a standard psychophysiological indicator of the amount of emotional arousal momentarily evoked. These reactions can be easily conditioned to a variety of stimuli, and to the best of our present knowledge, the individual has no voluntary control over them. GSR conditioning is usually accomplished by pairing a neutral stimulus with a painful one—for instance, electric shock. The purpose of Berger's experiment was to determine whether GSR conditioning can be accomplished through vicarious methods. Would the subject develop a conditioned emotional reaction to a neutral stimulus that apparently serves as a pain warning for another person?

In one of Berger's experiments vicarious conditioning was compared under two conditions. In both conditions all subjects were given ten vicarious conditioning trials and three test trials. In both conditions the subject was comfortably seated and GSR electrodes were strapped to his fingers. Another "subject," actually the experimenter's trained confederate, served as a "leader." On every vicarious conditioning trial a buzzer sounded; immediately afterward, a light dimmed; and immediately upon the dimming of the light, the experimenter's confederate—the leader—made a sharp movement with his hand.

The two conditions differed only in the ostensible cause of the leader's hand-movement. In the experimental condition, electrodes leading from an inductorium were strapped to the leader's hand. The subject was told that the "other subject" would be shocked every time the light dimmed. He was further told that the experimenter was concerned only with the subject's GSR to the buzzer and to the light, but that at the same time the experimenter was also interested in the "other subject's" GSR to electric shock. In the control condition, too, the leader jerked his hand when the light dimmed, but he was not strapped into the inductorium, and the subject was told that no shock would be given to either of them. In the control condition, the subject was further told that the experimenter was interested in the effects of the "other subject's" voluntary muscular movements on GSR.

In both conditions, on each of the ten vicarious conditioning trials, the buzzer sounded, the light dimmed, and the leader jerked his hand. On each of the three test trials the buzzer sounded, but the light did not dim, and the leader did not jerk his hand.

The results of Berger's experiment are shown in Figure 7, which

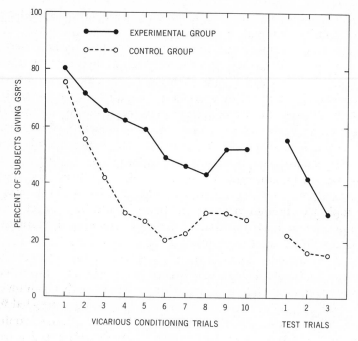

Figure 7

Galvanic skin reactions during and after the completion or vicarious conditioning. (Redrawn from Berger, 1962, with permission of author and publisher.)

plots the percentage of subjects who gave a galvanic skin reaction on each of the ten vicarious conditioning trials and on the three test trials. And we note that during the vicarious conditioning series, the experimental subjects showed considerably greater GSR reactivity than the control subjects did. This greater reactivity is maintained for the three test trials as well. The differences in GSR's between the two groups during vicarious conditioning must be interpreted to mean that sight of another person in pain is a *sufficient* stimulus for the arousal of an emotional response, since the only difference between the two conditions depended on whether or not the subject was led to believe that his partner was being shocked

Why did the experimental subjects maintain greater GSR reactivity for the three test trials? We are dealing here with something quite similar to classical conditioning. The leader's arm movement together with the dimming of the light may be thought of as the UCS (unconditioned stimulus) for the vicarious learner. This UCS produces a strong UR (unconditioned response) but only when the subject believes that the movement is caused by a shock.

A weak UR occurs when the model's movement is believed to be voluntary. The UR is in the form of an emotional response, measured by the Galvanic Skin Reaction. The buzzer, on the other hand, constitutes the subject's CS (conditioned stimulus). The results of the three test trials clearly show that the subject learned to react to the buzzer *alone:* he acquired a conditioned response. As a consequence of the repeated pairing of the buzzer with the sight of a person in pain, the buzzer itself began to evoke the strong emotional reaction previously brought about only by the sight of the person in pain.

CONFORMITY

In one of the most disturbing discoveries of social psychology, Solomon Asch (1962) found conclusive evidence that adult human subjects imitated a judgment that they knew was contrary to facts, contrary to what they perceived, or both. Moreover, Asch obtained this imitation of false judgments without reinforcing the "models" for their responses and without reinforcing the subject for his. Asch undertook his studies to understand better the intellectual dependence of man on society, which he felt to be one of the crucial moral dilemmas of our times. He expressed himself quite pointedly:

. . . In society we become dependent on others for understanding, feeling and the extension of the sense of reality. But this relation places a particular demand upon the participants of social action. If our dependence and trust are to have solid ground . . . , each must contribute out of his understanding and feeling. Often this condition is not fulfilled. The story of the emperor's new clothes is one example of baseless consensus produced by the failure of each to make his proper contribution. . . . We are appalled by the spectacle of the pitiful women of the Middle Ages who, accused of being witches by authorities they never questioned, confessed in bewilderment to unthought-of crimes. But in lesser measure we have each faced denials of our feelings and needs. . . . A theory of social influences must take into account the pressures upon persons to act contrary to their beliefs and values. . . . We need to go beyond the mild and painless aspects of group influence . . . (pp. 450–451).[1]

In one of Asch's experiments, subjects—adult college students—were required to compare the length of a "standard" line with one of three "comparison" lines. Both the standard and the comparison lines were in plain sight of the subjects, and the judgments were relatively easy. The length of the standard line varied from 1 to 9 inches. Among the three comparison lines, one was always the same length as the standard. The other two comparison lines differed from the standard by ¼ to 2½ inches.

When he entered the experimental room, the subject was told that his task, like that of the several other students present, would be to find for each "standard" line the matching one among the "comparison" lines. Unknown to the naive subject, the other seven or eight students were experimenter's confederates and had been previously instructed what response to make on each trial. The entire session consisted of twelve trials. On seven of these trials the confederates, who always made their judgments first, would unanimously select a wrong comparison line, sometimes differing from the standard by as much as 1¾ inches. Of course, all judgments were made orally, and the experimenter wrote them down after each trial. The experimental design also contained a control group of subjects, who made their judgments freely in the absence of confederates.

The results of Asch's experiment were astounding. In the absence of a false majority, subjects were able to achieve about 93 percent accuracy in their judgments. However, subjects exposed to the false judgment of the experimenter's confederates reached only 67 percent of accuracy—a 26 percent drop. In subsequent experiments Asch had his confederates make false judgments departing from the truth quite obviously. For instance, on one of the trials the standard line was 10 inches long, and the three comparison lines were 3, 10, and 2 inches long respectively. The confederates were instructed to choose the 3-inch line as the "correct" match. On another trial their estimate was 4 inches off. Nevertheless, the results remained as before. Because the comparisons were now somewhat easier to make, the control group achieved 98 percent of accuracy. But again, the experimental subjects showed only 72 percent accuracy—or again a 26 percent drop.

We may also add that under some conditions neither the difficulty of judgments nor subjects' competence in making such judgments has a significant effect on "yielding." Blake, Helson, and Mouton (1956) required adult subjects to count metronome clicks varying in speed, mak-

[1] Solomon E. Asch, *Social Psychology*. Copyright © 1952; by permission of the author and Prentice-Hall, Inc., Englewood Cliffs, New Jersey.

ing the judgments more or less difficult. No effects on yielding to false majority were obtained as a function of the speed of the metronome. In an experiment with children, and also using the metronome task, Iscoe, Williams, and Harvey (1964) failed to obtain differential yielding as a function of the child's ability to count the metronome clicks when alone. Children who in independent tests proved to be accurate judges of metronome speed yielded as often as children who were less accurate. However, Suppes and Schlag-Rey (1962) found that conformity increases with the difficulty of judgments.

When subjects are allowed to make their judgments privately and are not required to announce them aloud, the amount of yielding goes down somewhat (Deutsch and Gerard, 1955), but it does not disappear. Furthermore, when the group of confederates includes one individual who consistently makes correct comparisons, the amount of yielding again goes down—although 13 percent yielding still occurs (Asch, 1952). When the experimenter himself indicates the correct comparison line after each trial, 12 percent yielding to the false majority occurred (Jones, Wells, and Torrey, 1958). However, 47 percent yielding was obtained without any feedback, and 60 percent when the experimenter pointed to the comparison stimulus chosen by his confederates. Strong tendency to conform is not limited to American college sophomores. Crutchfield (1954) reported that a group of fifty American military officers yielded 37 percent of the time, and that engineers, writers, scientists, and architects did not show a lesser tendency to conform. Milgram (1961), on the other hand, found between 50 percent and 75 percent of yielding among Norwegian students, and between 34 percent and 59 percent among French students.

Crutchfield (1955) and others have begun to isolate personality factors that might be associated with vulnerability to social influence. They found that some individuals are less vulnerable to outside pressure. But it is still cause for amazement and perhaps for concern that many adults with good vision can say that a 3-inch line is 10 inches long simply because eight other adults say so.

On the other hand, conformity, like imitation, has some important adaptive benefits. Scare one bird, and the whole flock will fly away. Each member of the flock need not be threatened individually. The survival value of such a process cannot be overlooked. Responding to the behavior of others may be less discriminating and less independent, but waiting for the appropriate cue could be disastrous. When you see flood victims fleeing the impending disaster, you need not wait for the flood to come to your doorstep before running away.

Imitation is a significant device in learning. The opportunity to imitate saves the imitator the trouble of selecting from the totality of the environmental stimulation the cues relevant to his behavior at the moment. Others accomplish this task for him. Imitation prompts us to make appropriate responses that otherwise might not be made. This is extremely important, for if one is to acquire a response tendency, the response must be repeatedly reinforced. In order for reinforcement to occur, the response must first be made. If a given response has a low probability of occurrence, it will have a low probability of being reinforced, and hence a low probability of being learned. Miller and Dollard (1941) note that

. . . imitation can greatly hasten the process of independent learning by enabling the subject to perform the first correct response sooner than he otherwise would. Imitation is particularly important when . . . the occurrence of the correct response would otherwise be exceedingly improbable (p. 217).[2]

In the next chapter, a study by Bandura and McDonald (1963) will dramatically show that the subject with a "model" to imitate sometimes learns more efficiently than he would from reinforcement alone.

[2] N. E. Miller and J. Dollard, *Social Learning and Imitation* (New Haven, Conn.: Yale University Press, 1941). Reprinted with permission of author and publisher.

A CASE OF TANTRUM CONTROL

Carl D. Williams of the University of Miami reported (1959) a case of a 21-month-old child who terrorized his family with persistent and annoying tantrums. The boy had been quite ill for the first 18 months of his life and required constant care. After gaining health he

. . . demanded the special . . . attention that had been given him over the many critical months. He enforced some of his wishes, especially at bedtime, by unleashing tantrum behavior to control the actions of his parents. The parents and an aunt took turns in putting him to bed. . . . If the parent left the bedroom . . . , S would scream and fuss until the parent returned. . . . If the parent began to read while in the bedroom, S would cry until the reading material was put down. The parents felt that S enjoyed his control over them and that he fought off going to sleep as long as he could. In any event, a parent was spending from one-half to two hours each bedtime just waiting in the bedroom until S went to sleep (p. 269).[1]

Finally, a simple procedure was used: ". . . a parent or the aunt put S to bed in a leisurely and relaxed fashion. After bedtime pleasantries the parent left the bedroom and closed the door. S screamed and raged, but the parent did not re-enter the room." Each day under this procedure the duration of the child's tantrum behavior was recorded. The results over a 10-day period, beginning with the change in the parents' strategy, are shown in Figure 8. There is no question that the treatment was fully successful. On the first day, the child screamed for 45 minutes, but by the seventh day the tantrum behavior disappeared completely. Except for a brief recurrence of bedtime crying, which was rapidly eliminated by the same methods, the child ceased to terrorize his family. Williams found ". . . no unfortunate side- or after-effects of this treatment. . . . At three and three-quarters years of age, S appeared to be a friendly, expressive, outgoing child."

What we see in Figure 8 is a typical extinction curve. There are three basic ways of extinguishing a response pattern: (1) by withdrawing positive reinforcement, (2) by administering negative reinforcement,

---

[1] Williams, 1959; reprinted with permission of author and publisher.

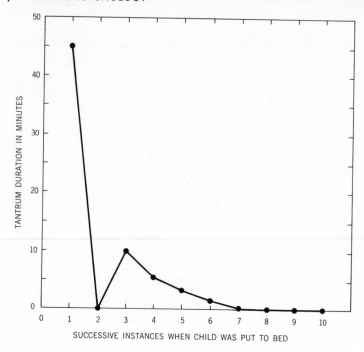

Figure 8

The extinction of tantrum behavior. (From Williams, 1959; redrawn with permission of author and publisher.)

or (3) by training new strong responses incompatible with the undesirable ones. No particular imagination is required to see that the child's tantrums were extinguished by the withdrawal of positive reinforcement. The point of this experiment is that either the presence of the parent or some of his actions previously served as reinforcements and, therefore, *controlled* the child's tantrum behavior.[2]

Up to now, we have considered only social *facilitation* or *inhibition* effects—how "others" enhance or impair *an already ongoing behavior* of the individual. But because others can administer reinforcement, they can also control the *direction* of the individual's behavior. Others provide

---

[2] That this idea is not particularly new or original is evident from the following eighteenth-century quotation: "If a child is so delicate and sensitive as naturally to resort to crying, I at once dry up the source of his tears by making them useless and without effect. As long as he is crying, I do not go to him; but I run to him the moment he has become still. Very soon, his way of calling me will be to cease crying, or at least to utter but one cry" (J.J. Rousseau, *Émile*, Book II.)

the reinforcements that help to control much of our behavior—including the reinforcements that satisfy our basic biological needs, such as hunger, thirst, and sex. Such reinforcements under the control of others are called *social reinforcements*.

In the Williams report, social reinforcement *maintained* the tantrum, and later—when reinforcement was withdrawn—the tantrum was *extinguished*. The same type of social reinforcement can also cause a child to acquire a proneness to tantrums. For example, a child and mother are at a fair. They are tired and irritated by the heat of the day. Suddenly, the child sees the stand selling cotton candy and asks for some. The mother flatly refuses. The child, fatigued already and now frustrated, begins to cry. The mother tells the child that she will not give in. The child cries louder. She asks him to stop. He doesn't. She asks again— now less gently. He still doesn't stop, so she slaps him. Then he screams, falls to the ground, and kicks—a full-blown tantrum. The embarrassed mother gives in and buys the cotton candy, and thus ends the tantrum. But by buying the candy just then she administered the first reinforcement. The tantrums are more likely to occur in the future now that the child has learned that screaming, especially in public, will get him what he wants.

In principle, almost any behavior can be acquired, maintained, and extinguished by means of carefully planned social reinforcement. Almost any behavior can *serve* as a social reinforcement, but most social reinforcement consists of practically effortless actions. A head nod, an "mm-hmm" often suffice. Let us look at some experimental evidence on this point.

Greenspoon (1955) asked his subjects to emit words at random for 50 minutes. Each time the subject came up with a plural word, the experimenter would say "mm-hmm"; and each time the subject came up with a singular word, he would say "huh-uh." In another group of subjects, "mm-hmm" reinforced a singular word, and "huh-uh" reinforced plural words. In both groups of subjects, "huh-uh" significantly decreased frequency of emission, and "mm-hmm" increased it.

More recently, Centers (1963) conducted an extensive investigation on the control of a casual everyday conversation by means of simple verbal reinforcements. Reinforcements of all sorts were used, including head nods, agreements, warm smiles, the verbalizations "yes," "I see," "uh-huh," etc. The execution of the experiment was quite ingenious. The subject was told to wait for the "experimenter" in the lobby of the psychological laboratory. While he waited, the experimenter's trained confederate—who looked and behaved like a subject—engaged him in conversation. Concealed microphones collected the critical data. When the "experimenter" finally came, the session was over, and the subjects were told the full story. But during the conversation the experimenter's confederate attempted to manipulate by means of social reinforcement: (a) the total amount of verbalization, (b) statements conveying some information, (c) statements of opinion and belief, and (d) questions. Before the confederate actually administered any reinforcement, the individual's operant level (the rate at which the individual normally verbalized, conveyed information, expressed opinions, and asked questions) was measured for 10 minutes. A second 10-minute period was devoted to measuring reinforcement effects, while the confederate dispensed reinforcement according to a previously agreed-upon schedule. The last 10 minutes constituted extinction training, when all positive reinforcement was withdrawn, and the confederate either stayed silent or disagreed with the subject. Response rates of the four types were again carefully measured. Of course, the subjects were not aware that measurements of their verbal output were being taken. These measurements, like those of the operant level, were actually made afterward from a tape obtained by recording the subject's conversation over the concealed microphones.

Figure 9 shows the average number of responses that the subjects emitted during the three phases of the experimental session. It is clear that social reinforcement constituted an extremely effective control of the conversational output of the subjects. All classes of verbal behavior, except "questions," showed significant increases over the subjects' operant (normal) level when the confederate dispensed reinforcement, and all these classes without exception significantly decreased during extinction when the confederate withdrew reinforcement. During extinction, responding reached an extremely low level—about 20 percent of the pre-reinforcement level—but no subjects became aware of what was happening.

Individuals can be influenced by the "mm-hmm" type of social reinforcement for many other types of verbalizations. Adams and Hoffman (1960) have worked with statements that subjects made about themselves while ostensibly being interviewed about student opinions. Whenever the subject began his statement with "I," "me," "mine," "myself," etc., he received an "mm-hmm" from the experimenter. Such self-reference statements markedly increased as a function of verbal reinforcement.

Greenspoon, Centers, and Adams and Hoffman attempted to control, by means of reinforcement only, *how much a person will talk.* But it is also possible to control to a large extent *what a person will say.* Hildum and Brown (1956) conducted a telephone "survey" on the Harvard philosophy of general education. In one group of interviews, whenever the respondent expressed himself in favor of the philosophy, the "inter-

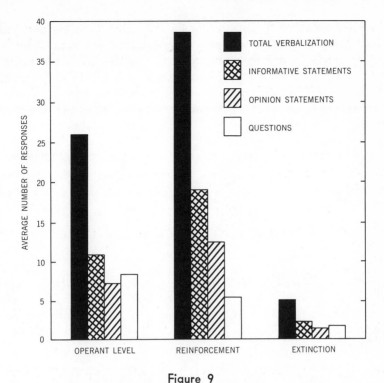

Figure 9

The reinforcement and extinction of verbal behavior.
(From Centers, 1963.)

viewer" would say "good." In another group he would say "good" only
if the respondent expressed himself negatively about the Harvard philosophy. The group that was reinforced for a positive attitude expressed
a greater number of favorable opinions than the group reinforced for
the negative attitude.

Besides demonstrating that simple reinforcement affects expressions
of opinions, the Hildum and Brown study also showed that a grave hazard
in public-opinion polling is the poll-taker himself. Before the interview,
the poll-taker's behavior must be thoroughly examined for any possibility
of biasing the answers of his respondents. In 1942 Professor Katz of the
University of Michigan found that working-class interviewers obtained
more favorable interviews on labor questions than white-collar interviewers. And Cantril (1944) reported that in a pre-election poll pro-
Democratic interviewers obtained more pro-Democratic interviews than
pro-Republican interviewers, and *vice versa.*

Singer (1961) demonstrated even more dramatically the effects of
social reinforcement on the expression of opinions. Singer had his subjects

fill out the so-called F-scale while he dispensed reinforcement under controlled conditions. The F-scale (F for fascism) was constructed by a group of California psychologists (Adorno, Frenkel-Brunswick, Levinson, and Sanford, 1950) for the purpose of isolating individuals with authoritarian and anti-democratic tendencies. The scale is widely used in psychological research, and subjects are asked whether they agree with such items as:

AN INSULT TO OUR HONOR SHOULD ALWAYS BE PUNISHED

SEX CRIMES, SUCH AS RAPE AND ATTACKS ON CHILDREN, DESERVE MORE THAN MERE IMPRISONMENT—SUCH CRIMINALS SHOULD BE PUBLICLY WHIPPED OR WORSE

PEOPLE DON'T PLACE ENOUGH EMPHASIS ON RESPECT FOR AUTHORITY

Singer selected sixty items from the F-scale for his purpose. Another thirty items, from the so-called E-scale, were also used in the study. The E-scale, constructed by the psychologists who constructed the F-scale, measures ethnocentric tendencies highly correlated with the authoritarian ones. Two items of the E-scale are:

EUROPEAN REFUGEES MAY BE IN NEED, BUT IT WOULD BE A BIG MISTAKE TO LOWER OUR EMIGRATION QUOTAS AND ALLOW THEM TO FLOOD THE COUNTRY

THE NEGROES WOULD SOLVE MANY OF THEIR SOCIAL PROBLEMS BY NOT BEING SO IRRESPONSIBLE, LAZY, AND IGNORANT

Agreement with these two items indicates a high degree of ethnocentrism. The experimenter called subjects in to the laboratory one by one. He then read the items, asking each time whether the subject agreed or disagreed with it. In the experimental group every time the student endorsed an antiauthoritarian item, or disagreed with an authoritarian item, the experimenter said "good" or "right." In the control group no reinforcement was given. This procedure was followed for the sixty F-scale items. Immediately afterward, the subjects were given thirty E-scale items, but now the reinforcement in both groups was withdrawn. Figure 10 shows Singer's results. Comparison of the F-scale endorsement of experimental and control groups showed a gradual but steady rise in pro-democratic responses during the acquisition series (F-scale items), and an equally consistent decline of these responses during extinction

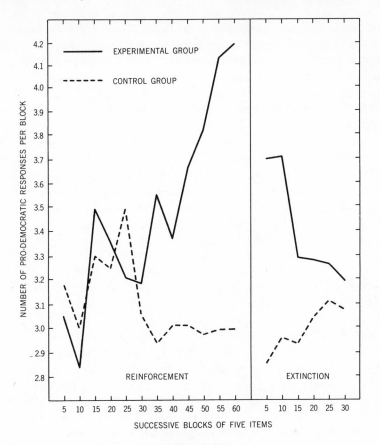

Figure 10

The effect of reinforcement on pro-democratic responses. (From Bandura and McDonald. Redrawn with permission of the authors and publisher.)

(E-scale items), reaching the prereinforcement (operant) level at the end of the session.

The experimental and control groups in Singer's experiment were initially matched for their scores on the F- and E-scales, both taken several months prior to the experiment proper. Under the influence of such seemingly trivial acknowledgment as "good" or "right," the experimental subjects made considerable gains in the pro-democratic and anti-authoritarian direction. At the outset of the acquisition series the experimental and control groups were endorsing on the average 3.1 or 3.2 items of the F-scale out of 5. Of the last 5 items, however, the reinforced subjects endorsed 4.2 while the controls remained at their operant level. This represents a gain of about 30 percent for a group of subjects who pride themselves on their budding intellectual integrity: all were students at an Ivy League university, and all were enrolled in an introductory psychology course.

Such reinforcement techniques as "mm-hmm," "good," "right," "fine," head nod, smile, and agreement are not simply *signals* for a given type of behavior. They are indeed *reinforcers*. When a physical signal, such as a buzzer, is substituted for the given verbal reinforcement, verbal output is not affected. For instance, Taffel (1955), using the reinforcement "good," increased the frequency with which his subjects constructed sentences with the pronouns "I" and "we," but Taffel could not increase pronoun usage by means of a light signal. And Anne Nuthmann (1957) found significant reinforcement effects on responses "accepting of self" by using "good" but could not obtain them by means of a light signal. The subjects were given items such as I AM SOMETIMES SHY AND UNSURE IN THE PRESENCE OF STRANGERS to endorse. Subject's agreement with items asserting a weakness was defined as "self-acceptance" and was reinforced.

Many of our habits, values, and beliefs are taught to us by our parents. It is meaningful, therefore, to inquire just how effective is reinforcement given by one's own parents, as compared to that given by strangers, for instance. There is only scant evidence on this subject. Stevenson, Keen, and Knights (1963) compared the performance of preschool children on a simple gamelike task (placing marbles into holes) when parents and strangers controlled the children's responses with reinforcement such as "That's very good" and "You're really good at this game." Strangers produced a significantly greater increase in response rates of the children.

SOCIAL REINFORCEMENT AND IMITATION: A PROBLEM OF THE RELATIVE EFFICACY OF LEARNING

We saw in the preceding chapter that learning can be considerably enhanced when the learner imitates a skilled performer or observes another's learning process. In this chapter we have considered the role of social reinforcement in behavior. Both imitation and social reinforcement were found to be extremely powerful controls of behavior, but which is more efficient? An ingenious study by Bandura and McDonald (1963) compared the learning of moral judgments under direct reinforcement and imitation. Bandura and McDonald constructed thirty-six pairs of stories, ". . . each of which described a well-intentioned act which resulted in considerable damage, contrasted with a selfishly or maliciously motivated act producing minor consequences." Twelve of the story pairs were given to a group of children, 5 to 11 years old. The children were to judge for each pair which was ". . . the naughtier thing." On the basis of this pretest they were divided into two smaller groups, one with a strong *subjective* orientation, and another with an *objective* orientation. These two classifications derive from the theory of the Swiss psychologist Jean Piaget (1948) who hypothesized that children develop a moral sense in an irreversible sequence of changes. According to this theory, children under seven tend to view a harmful act by its consequences—that is, by the amount of damage it has caused (the objective stage). Older children evaluate such acts by their antecedents—that is, by the intent of the person responsible for the act (subjective stage).

One to three weeks after pretest the experimental manipulations were carried out. Each group was divided into three experimental conditions. In all conditions the child was again asked to make similar moral judgments on twelve pairs of stories. In Condition I the children's judgments were preceded by those of an adult "model," who was the experimenter's confederate instructed to choose always the alternative opposite to the child's own orientation. In this condition the "model" was reinforced for all his responses and the child was reinforced for imitating him—which meant, of course, that the child was only reinforced for making judgments contrary to his own orientation. The experimenter reinforced him by saying "very good," "that's fine," etc. Condition II was identical in all respects, except that the child was not reinforced at all. In Condition III the child made judgments alone in the absence of a model and was reinforced as in Condition I—that is, for judgments opposite to his own orientation. To determine the stability of the effects, the twelve remaining pairs of stories were given to the children after the conditioning was terminated and under the same conditions as in pretest.

The results of Bandura and McDonald's study are unmistakably clear. We see in Figure 11 that in the pretest stage all groups of children are about even. The subjectively oriented children make an average of 20 percent of objective judgments, and the objectively minded subjects around 17 or 18 percent of subjective judgments. In the presence of a model, both groups of children reversed their judgments by more than 30 percent. But more important is the finding that this effect is independent of social reinforcement. The presence of a model is equally effective for children who were reinforced for reversing their orientation as for those who received no reinforcement whatever. Moreover, social reinforcement by itself (Condition III) has no effect on subjectively oriented children, and its effect is relatively weak for the objectively oriented children (about 15 to 16 percent). The post-test (extinction test) data show that the effects of the model remain stable (Conditions I and II), while the social-reinforcement effects (Condition III) obtained

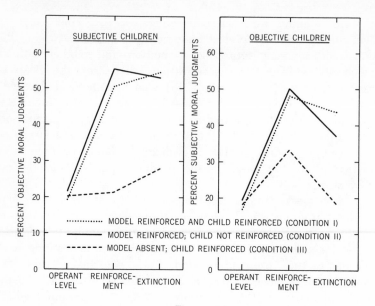

Figure 11

Reinforcement and extinction of children's moral sponses. (From Bandura and McDonald; redrawn with permission of authors and publisher.)

for the objectively minded subjects immediately disappear. For some tasks, therefore, imitation is a necessary *and* sufficient condition for learning, while social reinforcement is certainly not necessary and hardly sufficient.

Why is the imitation training of the Bandura-McDonald subjects so much superior to a method using social reinforcement? As noted at the end of Chapter 4, under operant conditioning procedures, in contrast to classical conditioning, reinforcement is given *only* when the subject *emits* the conditioned response. If the normal operant rate of the response to be conditioned is low, the individual will simply have little opportunity to receive reinforcement, and consequently he will have little opportunity to learn. The operant rates in the Bandura-McDonald study were between 17 and 20 percent (see Figure 11). The chance of the child receiving reinforcement in Condition III was, therefore, one out of five or six. Since there were only twelve trials in the acquisition series, he could be reinforced on the average only twice or three times during the entire training session. The presence of a model prompts the child to emit these low-probability responses and affords him therefore with a greater opportunity of receiving reinforcement for emitting the responses.

PART TWO

SOCIAL
INTERACTION

In Part I we were concerned with the behavior of a single individual as it is influenced by others. We found that they can influence his behavior (1) by modifying his general drive state, as in audience or coaction effects; (2) by providing him with cues for appropriate and correct responses, as in imitation, vicarious learning, or conformity; or (3) by dispensing reinforcement. The analysis of social behavior has been organized in this book according to these three classes of antecedent variables, which correspond to three fields of general psychology: motivation, perception, and learning (see Chapter 1, pp. 1–2).

The three foci of analysis of social behavior can be schematically represented as follows:

$$(1) \qquad R_j \longrightarrow D_i \longrightarrow R_i.$$
$$(2) \qquad R_j \longrightarrow S_i \longrightarrow R_i.$$
$$(3) \qquad R_j \longrightarrow K_i \longrightarrow R_i.$$

D denotes motivational variables; S, perceptual variables; and K, reinforcement variables. R_i denotes the response of a given individual, i; R_j denotes the responses of another individual, j. The arrows mean "influences," "causes," or "occasions the occurrence of."

The first focus of analysis, (1), defines the experimental paradigms we examined in Chapters 2 and 3; the responses of a given individual, R_i, are modified by a change in his own motivational state, D_i, which in turn is modified by the responses of another individual or individuals, R_j. The second focus of analysis, (2), represents the experimental paradigm of imitation, vicarious learning, and conformity; the responses of a given individual are controlled by a set of cues, S_i, produced by the responses of a "leader" or a "model." The third focus of analysis of social behavior, (3), represents the paradigm of social reinforcement; the responses of a given individual are modified by means of reward and punishment, K_i, which in turn are produced or controlled by the responses of another individual.

As we noted in Chapter 1 (p. 1), *social interaction* is the mutual and reciprocal case of social behavior. In this case at least two individuals are considered, and we are interested not only in the influence of individual j on i, but also in the influence of i on j. Since social behavior was defined in terms of behavioral dependence, social interaction is naturally defined in terms of behavioral *inter*dependence. We will also analyze social interaction in three foci corresponding to three fields of general psychology: motivation, perception, and learning.

The following paradigm illustrates motivational interdependence:

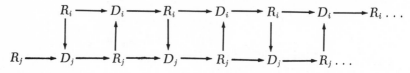

where the letters, the arrows, and the subscripts have the same meaning as previously. In this paradigm, the motivational or arousal states of two individuals change over time, as a function of their responses to each other. A typical example is the interaction among mating mammals. Each is capable of increasing and decreasing the other's sexual drive level. The female in heat, her mating drive highly aroused, attracts a mate, whose sexual drive becomes aroused largely as a consequence of her responses. The male's behavior, in turn, further increases her motivation to mate. And the sexual motivation of both organisms returns to its latent state ofter the consummatory act. Such motivational interdependence exists to some extent in all types of interaction among individuals.[1]

A paradigm similar to the one for motivational interdependence can be used to illustrate perceptual interdependence:

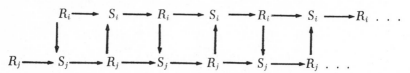

It is perhaps obvious that we are dealing here with *communication*. The responses of one individual are the cues for the responses of the other, which in turn become cues for the responses of the first. Cues are by definition "carriers" of information, and transmission of information is the essence of communication. A good deal of work has been accomplished in research on communication, and we shall be concerned in this part of the book with various aspects of this research.

---

[1] There is very little experimental work on motivational interdependence, and we shall not pursue the matter in detail. The student interested in this field is referred to the work of Lewis (1944), Horwitz (1954), and Zander and Medow (1963). An ingenious mathematical treatment of motivational interdependence is due to Rapoport (1947a, 1947b).

Behavioral interdependence can also be analyzed with an emphasis upon reinforcement reciprocity. Two alternative paradigms illustrate reinforcement interpendence:

$$(1) \quad \begin{array}{c} R_i - + \to K_i - + \to R_i - + \to K_i - + \to R_i - + \to K_i - + \to R_i \ldots \\[6pt] R_j - + \to K_j - + \to R_j - + \to K_j - + \to R_j - + \to K_j - + \to R_j \ldots \end{array}$$

$$(2) \quad \begin{array}{c} R_i - + \to K_i - + \to R_i - + \to K_i - + \to R_i - + \to K_i - + \to R_i \ldots \\[6pt] R_j - + \to K_j - + \to R_j - + \to K_j - + \to R_j - + \to K_j - + \to R_j \ldots \end{array}$$

The positive arrows mean "promotes," "fosters," etc., while the negative arrows mean "hinders," "inhibits," "prevents," etc. Paradigm (1) illustrates *cooperation:* cooperating individuals produce responses that constitute or lead to positive mutual reinforcement (indicated by plus signs): Paradigm (2) illustrates *competition:* competing individuals produce responses that lead to negative mutual reinforcement or to the prevention of positive mutual reinforcement (indicated by minus signs). Viewed in this manner, *conflict* between individuals is a special case of competition.

The above paradigms do not define social interaction uniquely or exhaustively. To avoid complexity, we have limited the analysis of behavioral interdependence to the case of only two individuals. Furthermore, social interaction does not *primarily* involve *either* motivational *or* cue *or* reinforcement interdependence. Social interaction involves all three forms in amounts varying from situation to situation. These forms may not exist in a separate, strictly concrete sense; and there may be more than three forms of social interaction. We have arbitrarily chosen abstract processes that will simplify our study in Part II.

6

COMMUNICATION AND SOCIAL LIFE

The female phalarope, a small wading bird of the Arctic, has few of the usual maternal responsibilities. After laying the eggs, she considers her duty fulfilled, and leaves the future of the offspring entirely to her mate. The male incubates the eggs and brings up the young, staying with them long after the unscrupulous female has gone. But the male must somehow learn *when* he will assume his paternal responsibilities. He also must somehow learn the whereabouts of the eggs. When the time comes, either he selects the nest site and shows the female where to lay eggs, or she selects it and shows it to him. In either case some *information must be transmitted between the couple*. Niko Tinbergen, the Dutch naturalist who studied these Arctic birds quite extensively, made the following observations (1958) on the communication process among them:

Our female acquired a mate in due course; the birds lived and foraged together, and copulated several times. Now and then the female went on land and made a "scrape" by sitting down and scrabbling backward with the feet in the same way as other waders do. Usually the male joined her and soon the birds had made a number of scrapes at various places near the pond. Some of them they visited more than once, others seemed to be forgotten soon after they had been made.

One day, while the two birds were quietly foraging on the pool, the female suddenly uttered her "song"—which we had not heard since she had acquired a mate—and flew up. But instead of landing on the water, she flew into the marsh and went to a scrape. The male followed her at once, which he did not usually do when she flew off, and together they busied themselves there for a couple of minutes. All at once the female sang again, flew off once more, again taking the male with her. She now went to another scrape. And in this way the pair went from one scrape to another . . . In the fourth scrape the female stayed a little longer and there she laid her first egg.

I was particularly struck by this revival of the song and by the male's prompt response to it. I missed the laying of the second egg because a gale prevented me from crossing the fjord. The next day, expecting the bird to lay her third egg, I took no chances and kept a continuous watch on the pair from 1.15 A.M. I expected to see her lay her third egg some time early that morning. As it turned out I had to keep up my vigil until 5 P.M., when the birds rewarded me by going through exactly the same ceremony again.

I was so pleased to see this because it confirmed, in a way, the general biological "philosophy" which is behind so much of a naturalist's watching. I understood that this bird *had* to have something like this ceremony and that the male *had* to follow the female so promptly . . . Obviously the "nest-showing" ceremony was the means by which the female made the male follow her to where she would lay the eggs, so that he could learn their whereabouts (pp. 66–64).[1]

Besides revealing the remarkable patience and dedication of the naturalist, the above passage illustrates with a most dramatic simplicity the role of communication in social life. If female phalaropes were incapable of informing their mates of the location of eggs, these eggs might never hatch, and phalaropes might simply not survive as a species.

All species have some means of communication. Not all of these means are known today, but it is only a matter of scientific ingenuity to discover them. The communication process among bees, for instance, was first discovered by the German zoologist Karl von Frisch in 1923. He noticed that when a foraging honeybee returns to the hive after locating food he performs a curious waggling dance on the vertical surface of the honeycomb. During this dance its abdomen describes the figure eight, whose orientation indicates the direction of the food source. The speed of the dance—that is, the number of revolutions per minute— is directly related to the distance of the food source from the hive. Other bees "receive" this information by touching the dancer with their antennae. Werner (1964) found that the dancer emits a low-frequency sound, whose duration is also directly related to the distance of the food source from the hive. Since the interior of the hive is dark, these auditory signals are in all probability very necessary elements of the communication process among bees.

Evidence about efficient and meaningful communication among animals has recently been obtained in laboratory experiments. One of the important contributions in this field is due to Murphy, Miller, and Mirsky (1955), who developed an ingenious technique for training primates to respond to each other under controlled conditions. In one of a series of studies based on this technique, Miller, Banks, and Ogawa (1962) first trained rhesus monkeys to avoid shock by pressing a lever. A monkey was strapped in a chair equipped with a stimulus display (which consisted of a light signal), a source of electric shock, and a bar that served as the off-switch for the shock circuit when depressed. To adapt the animals to this rather restrictive environment, each animal was kept strapped in the chair for five days without being shocked. At the end of the adaptation period, spontaneous bar-pressing was measured

[1] Tinbergen, 1958; reprinted with permission of author and publisher.

to determine the free operant rate. Then avoidance conditioning began. In each conditioning trial, a light was turned on for six seconds; when the light went off, an electric shock would be administered if the monkey had not pressed the bar during the six-second "light" period. The shock continued until the monkey responded. If the animal did emit the appropriate avoidance response during the "light" period, he would not receive a shock.

Two animals, trained separately, received 200 such avoidance conditioning trials. After the completion of training both animals were able to avoid shock about 95 percent of the time. The two primate chairs were then placed face-to-face so that the animals could see but not touch each other. The stimulus display was removed from one chair, leaving that animal with just the response bar. The response bar was removed from the other chair, leaving the second animal with just the stimulus display. Now only one animal would receive the conditioning stimulus (light) and only one could perform the conditioned response (bar pressing). The problem confronting the animals was tricky:

The monkey with the light had no means of performing the instrumental response which would avoid the noxious shock stimulus. The second monkey could perform the response but had no stimulus to inform him when a response was appropriate. However, if the animal with the stimulus was able to *communicate* [2] to his partner . . . that the conditioned stimulus (CS) was being presented, the second monkey could then make the appropriate instrumental response which would enable both animals to avoid the shock (Miller, Banks, and Ogawa, 1962).

The interdependent monkeys were observed for twenty-two days and received twenty trials each day. On the first day of testing the monkeys avoided the shock on only three of the twenty occasions. But already on the second test day, the number of avoidances increased to seventeen, remaining at that level on the third day, and rising to nineteen (that is 95 percent of success) on the fourth day. During the first eight days of training, successful avoidance was due largely to an unusually high rate of responding on the part of the monkey with the bar, who continued pressing it even when the stimulus light was not turned on for his partner. From the eighth day on, however, the monkey with the bar responded primarily when the other monkey was exposed to the conditioned stimulus.

On the sixteenth day of testing a wooden partition was inserted between the two monkeys, exposing only their heads. The presence of the partition did not visibly change the ability of the animals to avoid shock. On the twenty-third day and for three days thereafter the animals were

[2] Italics mine.

given some individual reconditioning trials. The roles of the two monkeys were then reversed: the one previously supplied with the stimulus display now received only the bar, while the monkey previously responsible for the execution of the avoidance response was now provided only with the stimulus display. Testing continued for ten consecutive days, again with twenty trials each day. During this period there were 190 successful avoidances out of the 200 possible. Again a half screen, and later a full screen, were inserted between the primate chairs toward the end of testing. Avoidance was no less effective even when the animals were completely concealed from each other. The authors report that the animal with the "stimulus panel frequently squirmed and slapped at his chair when the stimulus was being presented."

After the conclusion of this experiment, a new monkey was selected to replace the one equipped only with the light. This new monkey *had no previous avoidance conditioning*. Could the naive partner communicate to the sophisticated animal that the light was on, so that the sophisticated animal could prevent the shock?

Tests were performed for fourteen consecutive days, and successful avoidance—significantly greater than chance—began to appear on the fourth day of testing. Again neither half screen nor full screen affected the efficiency of communication that must have been taking place. On the fifteenth day the roles were switched as before, and again the animals were observed for the avoidance of shock. Learning was very rapid. On the second day the animals showed a significant avoidance behavior, and only seventeen out of 200 trials were unsuccessful. Of these, thirteen occurred on the first day.

Miller, Banks, and Ogawa could not establish in their study whether any significant vocalizations occurred, but it should not be very hard to analyze this possibility. Using the approach of the Miller, Banks, and Ogawa experiments, resarchers can now begin to isolate the parameters of interanimal communication in detail and systematically. They can restrict the channels of communication between two animals, cutting them off from each other's vision, restricting the sounds they can produce artificially (banging on the chair, for example), and ultimately filtering the animals' vocalization. A systematic program of research using this method may eventually provide us with an understanding of the monkeys' "language."

Observing the behavior of the *communicator* and of the *receiver*, Miller, Banks, and Ogawa developed a procedure which will eventually enable us to analyze the *messages* that the communicator transmits to the receiver. It is convenient to divide the analysis of communication according to these three abstract elements: the behavior of the communicator, the behavior of the receiver, and the type of messages exchanged between them. The analysis of messages is not within the direct competence of psychology, and we shall not consider it here.[3]

BEHAVIOR OF THE COMMUNICATOR

In order to understand the behavior of the communicator it is first useful to inquire *why* he communicates at all. What factors determine whether an individual will transmit some information to another individual? To answer this question, we will distinguish among three types of communication: *incidental, consummatory,* and *instrumental.*

In *incidental* communication the communicator imparts information to another without having any intention of doing so, and often, without any knowledge that he does so. A dog barking at the milkman inadvertently signals his own presence to neighbor dogs, chipmunks, rabbits, cats, humans, etc. By cues varying in subtlety, people communicate their background, interests, wants and needs, knowledge and ignorance, and a host of other information—without having the slightest inclination of doing so, and often in spite of a definite desire for concealment.

The distinction between consummatory and instrumental communication was first made by Festinger (1950). *Consummatory* communication arises as a consequence of an emotional or motivational state of the individual (joy, grief, fear, and so on), and it is merely the expression of this state. *Instrumental* communication, on the other hand, is goal-directed. It seeks to achieve definite effects in the recipient, and it will vary directly with his reactions. If salt is not passed after the first request, the request is repeated. In consummatory communication, messages are *emitted;* their form and content depend only on the state of the communicator. In instrumental communication, messages are *transmitted,* and they vary according to the effects they are intended to produce in the receiver. Thus, for instance, in studying communication intended to achieve uniformity in groups, Festinger and his colleagues (1950) were able to make some predictions about what determines that a given message will be sent, who will receive it, and what effect it will have upon the receivers.

If there is in a group a pressure toward uniformity (for example, reaching a unanimous decision), and if communication is instrumental to the achievement of uniformity, then deviant group members should be the primary targets of communication. Festinger and Thibaut (1951) investigated this hypothesis, among others, by means of the following

[3] The two disciplines that deal with the analysis of messages are a branch of linguistics called *semiotic,* and a branch of mathematics called *information theory.* Semiotic is concerned with the rules and regularities in the construction of messages. Information theory, as the name implies, is the quantitative study of information carried by messages in general (see Fitts and Posner, 1966).

procedure. Groups of six to fourteen subjects were asked to consider a problem—for instance, the choice of a particular football strategy. Seven alternative solutions were provided, ranging from an extremely reckless play to an extremely conservative one. The group members, individually and privately, selected the solution they preferred. Each member's opinion was made public to the others. They were asked then to "discuss" the problem as a group. The participants, however, could "discuss" the solutions only through written notes, enabling the researchers to record and analyze the nature and traffic of messages more efficiently than would have been possible in an ordinary conversation.

Three degrees of pressure toward uniformity were created. In order to produce strong pressures the experimenter informed the groups that his interest "was in observing how groups went about coming to a unanimous decision." To produce medium pressures the experimenter told the groups he wanted to see how many individuals could find the correct solution. In the weak-pressure condition, the experimenter told the subjects he was interested "in observing the way a group went about discussing such a problem." Figure 12 shows that individuals proposing extreme solutions (that is, very reckless or very conservative

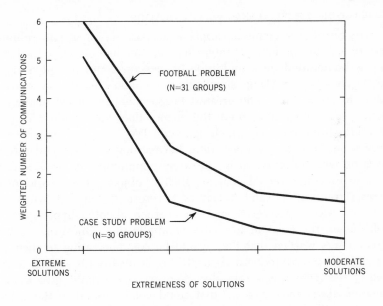

Figure 12

Amount of communication directed to persons proposing extreme and moderate solutions. (Festinger and Thibaut, 1951; redrawn with permission of author and publisher.)

plays) received five times as many messages as those advocating more moderate solutions. Moreover, when the three degrees of pressures toward uniformity were compared, it was found that communications to extremes increased with the amount of pressure. In a further experiment (Schachter, 1951) it was found that communication to extreme members ceases when they change their opinions. Moreover, if the group members perceive that communication will not change the deviant's position, communication to him stops, and he is virtually rejected from membership. These experiments, and others that derive from Festinger's original studies, show that by observing communication, inferences can be made about rather subtle group processes, such as uniformity pressures, potential rejection of members, cohesiveness, organization, etc.

BEHAVIOR OF THE RECEIVER

In considering the reception of messages we shall first examine the effects of receiving *instrumental* communication. Secondly, we shall look into the ability of individuals to understand and profit from *consummatory* communication of others. Finally, we shall inquire if *incidentally* produced information has any value.

RECEIVING INSTRUMENTAL COMMUNICATION

The receiver of communication is not passive, impartially admitting every bit of information that might happen to come his way. Each of us daily is bombarded by a multitude of messages, and our physiological and psychological makeup simply does not allow us to pay equal attention to all of them. The greatest proportion (an almost uncountable amount) is completely ignored. But chance does not decide which messages are admitted and which ignored. We "prepare" ourselves for information. Such preparatory states have strong selective and directive effects on what information is ultimately admitted or ignored, and how it is organized if received (Zajonc, 1960). Subjects in two experimental groups ("transmitters" and "receivers") were told that they would each be paired with a partner to make a decision about a hypothetical job applicant on the basis of his letter of application. One group ("transmitters") was warned that they would be communicating to their partners what they were to learn about the applicant from his letter. Another group ("receivers") was told that their partners would give them information about the applicant that could not be found in the letter of application. The identical letter of application was then given to both groups, and tests were run to determine how these "transmitters" and "receivers" organized information contained in it.

The preparatory state of a "transmitter" prompts him to receive and organize information in potential units of transmittable messages. The "transmitters" therefore pay attention to specific details of the letter in order to transmit them, item by item, in some meaningful sequence. The "receivers," however, tend to regard the information in the letter of application in rather broad categories that would later become instrumental in organizing further messages that they expect to receive from their future partners. Since the "receivers" do not really know what sort of information their partners might later have for them, these categories have to be sufficiently general to accommodate all sorts of material. When the subjects were actually tested for recall of the material in the letter of application—prior to any contact with their partners—the "transmitters" reported primarily specific information, while the "receivers" remembered primarily general information about the applicant. Moreover, the material remembered by the "transmitters" was more organized and more differentiated than that of the "receivers."

The preparatory state of the receiver does not depend only on what he expects to do with the information received. It also depends on who the communicator is, what opinion he holds, how reliable his information might be, and so forth. A variation of the above experiment examined the effects of a communicator's opinion. The procedure was repeated but now the subjects were asked to decide whether the applicant should be hired. Half of the subjects were then informed that they were to discuss their decisions with partners who had made the same decision as they; and the other half of the subjects were to be paired with partners who decided otherwise. Again, recall analysis showed that the anticipation of entering into communication with a person who holds a contrary opinion leads to a tighter organization of the received information, to an increased specificity of the units into which the material is broken up, and to a marked tendency to overselect items supporting one's own position.

The communication process will be efficient if the intent of the communicator and the preparatory state of the receiver are congruent. For instance, they must think of the subject matter in similar terms. Rumors are often distorted during transmission because the various persons who in turn receive and transmit them are not always "tuned in" for content in the same way. Haney (1964) traced the fate of a rumor, which he initiated and a chain of six students relayed. The statement that the first member of the chain received was:

Every year at State University, the eagles in front of the Psi Gamma fraternity house were mysteriously sprayed during the night. Whenever this happened, it cost the Psi Gams from $75 to $100 to have the eagles cleaned. The Psi Gams complained to officials and were promised by the president that if ever any student were caught painting the eagles, they would be expelled from school (p. 14).[4]

Some very bizarre transformations occurred in the story. But these transformations always made some sense, and showed internal consistency. In some of the groups, for instance, the final product was as follows:

At a State University there was an argument between two teams— the Eagles and the Fire Gems—in which their clothing was torn.

Or:

The eagles in front of the university had parasites and were sprayed with insecticide.

Or:

At State U. they have many birds which desecrate the buildings. To remedy the situation they expelled the students who fed the birds.

Runkel (1956) examined more extensively how congruence of the preparatory states of the communicators affects the efficiency of communication. Students in an introductory psychology course—and five teachers in the course—were asked to indicate the extent of their agreement with the following five assertions:

A. The conditions of living in the United States tend to narrow the range of things we are able to do, think, etc.
B. People who have a firm moral code are in general better adjusted than those who have not.
C. The biggest weakness of present-day psychology is that it is too theoretical.
D. Individuals could be changed practically any way one might wish if the environment could be appropriately controlled.
E. The strongest influence in shaping a person into the kind of person he becomes is his mother.

For each subject a rank order of the five statements was obtained, indicating his willingness to endorse them. Runkel was primarily interested in whether the student and his instructor considered these statements according to the same criteria and the same values, and what were the student's grades as a consequence of this correspondence. It is important to note, however, that the correspondence between the student's and instructor's criteria is not a matter of a positive correlation

[4] Haney, 1964; reprinted with permission of author and publisher.

between their respective rankings. Even if a student ranked the five above statements A, B, C, D, E, while his instructor ranked them E, D, C, B, A, the two were considered to have ordered the assertions according to the same underlying attribute—they would, in Runkel's words, be "co-linear" with one another.

The following example clarifies the notion of "co-linearity." New York, Detroit, Chicago, and Los Angeles differ in longitude and in size. Let us represent the longitude of these cities on the abscissa and their size on the ordinate of a graph. We can then plot the location of each city at the intersection of these two dimensions, as follows:

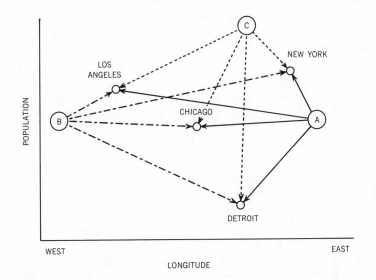

Three individuals—A, B, and C—rank these cities according to their preferences as places to settle:

A: New York, Detroit, Chicago, Los Angeles.
B: Los Angeles, Chicago, Detroit, New York.
C: New York, Chicago, Los Angeles, Detroit.

We can also speak of the individual as having a "location" in the graph. The location of A represents his "ideal" city, and it is indicated by a circle. It represents the exact longitude *and* population size he would most prefer. In general, the individual will rank the four cities according to the distance of each city from his "ideal." The closer the location of the city to the location of the ideal, the higher its rank in the preference order. Thus, A ranked his cities primarily in longitude, from east to west. B, on the other hand, ranked his cities from west to east. To both A and

B the size is not of great consequence. However, C prefers to live in as large a city as possible. His rank order does not discriminate the cities in terms of longitude—it discriminates them primarily in terms of size. We say then that the longitude is the attribute underlying the rankings of A and B, and size the attribute underlying the rankings of C. By definition, A and B are co-linear with one another, while the pairs A and C, and B and C, are not co-linear. (The student should take it for granted that it is possible to determine whether two rank orders are co-linear even if we do not know the underlying attributes.)

Runkel found that students who were co-linear with their instructors received significantly higher grades on a regular class quiz than students who were not. The instructor communicated during the semester more efficiently to students who structured information along dimensions and attributes like his. In other words, in a class taught by an instructor whose ranking was A, B, C, D, E, a student with ranking E, D, C, B, A had a greater chance for a good grade than a classmate with ranking A, B, D, C, E. Even though the latter student differs in his preferences from the instructor by only a one-step transposition, he is not co-linear with him.

RECEIVING CONSUMMATORY COMMUNICATION

We are all able to comprehend the emotional expressions of other people. We can see, with greater or lesser clarity, that someone is gay or angry or panic-stricken. We can recognize these emotional states in others better if they come from our own culture, and better still if they are expressed by someone whom we know well. These emotional expressions—examples of consummatory communication—have definite effects and value, even if they are not intended to produce them. The fear cry of a bird in danger may be simply expressing the bird's own feelings, yet it serves the useful function of alerting other birds to danger.

Miller, Banks, and Ogawa (1963) found that rhesus monkeys are able to communicate "meaning" through emotional expressions. A group of animals was first trained to perform an avoidance bar-pressing response to the conditioned stimulus consisting of auditory clicks. Six seconds after the clicks began the animals received an electric shock if they had not made the appropriate avoidance response. The clicks and the shock continued until the bar-pressing response was made. Toward the end of the training, the subjects averaged better than 90 percent success in avoiding the shock.

After the completion of the training, the monkeys were tested, two at a time in separate rooms, in a "cooperative learning" situation similar to the one in the previously described experiment (pp. 55–58). One member of each pair was deprived of the opportunity to make the avoidance response (his response bar was removed), while the other member was deprived of the conditioned stimulus (he was not exposed to the six seconds of clicks preceding the shock onset). This latter monkey, however, could see a television receiver that showed the face of his partner when he was exposed to the clicks and during the intervals between clicks as well. The monkeys who knew about the onset of the conditioned stimulus only from their partners' images on the television screen, were able to avoid shock successfully 89 percent of the time, which is about as well as they did when the conditioned stimulus was directly accessible to them. This means, of course, that the monkey's facial expressions alone carried to his partner, faithfully and accurately, the entire information about the onset of the clicks.

RECEIVING INCIDENTAL INFORMATION

Can incidentally overheard information help change an opinion? Allyn and Festinger (1961) examined this question in a rather clever experiment. Two groups of high school students were introduced to an "authority on driving," who delivered a scathing speech against teen-age drivers. (This amounted to an attack on a popular teen-age position.) Members of one group were told to listen carefully so they could answer questions later about the speech itself. Members of the other group were told to listen carefully so they could answer questions later about the speaker's personality. Measures of students' opinions about teen-age driving showed that those asked to pay attention to the speaker's personality changed their views in his direction considerably more than those "tuned in" on the subject matter itself.

Festinger and Maccoby (1964) give an interesting explanation of the Allyn-Festinger results:

. . . Let us first try to understand the cognitive behavior of a person who, strongly committed to an opinion, listens to a vigorous, persuasive communication that attacks that opinion. Certainly, such a listener is not passive. He does not sit there listening and absorbing what is said without any counteraction on his part. Indeed, it is most likely that under such circumstances, while he is listening to the persuasive communication, he is very actively, inside his own mind, counterarguing, derogating the points the communicator makes, and derogating the communicator himself. In other words, we can imagine that there is really an argument going on, one side being vocal and the other subvocal. Let us imagine that one could somehow prevent the listener from arguing back while listening to the persuasive communication. If one created such a passive listener, it seems reasonable to expect that the persuasive communication would then have more of an impact. The listener, not able to counterargue, would be more influenced and would be less likely to reject the communication. And perhaps this is exactly what was really done in the experiment reported by Allyn and Festinger (p. 360).[5]

In a further experiment designed to examine this hypothesis, Festinger and Maccoby compared several groups of students who heard an argument strongly advocating the abolition of fraternities. To all groups, the argument was presented on the same sound track. In some groups, the sound track was accompanied by the film of the speaker making the speech in question. In other groups, the sound track was accompanied by an absolutely irrelevant short film called *Day of the Painter*. In the latter groups, subjects were prevented from subvocally counterarguing the speaker's points, and were, therefore, expected to show more opinion change. They in fact did.

While we cannot generalize that incidental communication is always more effective in opinion change, such incidental communication may sometimes be significant. Soft sell may indeed be better than hard sell, and very soft sell better yet. But the circumstances under which incidental communication is especially effective in forming and changing opinions remain to be discovered.[6]

[5] Reprinted with permission of authors and publisher.
[6] For an extensive analysis of persuasion, see Hovland, Janis, and Kelley (1953).

COOPERATION, COMPETITION, AND CONFLICT

7

COOPERATION IN THE MINIMAL SOCIAL SITUATION

In the Miller-Banks-Ogawa experiments (1962, 1963) described in the last chapter, the reinforcement of each subject depended on the other's responses. The monkeys, however, *were able to cooperate only if they could communicate with one another*. These studies may have led the reader to believe erroneously that communication is an essential of cooperation. Communication does enhance cooperation, but the only requirement of the cooperative process, as sketched in the paradigm on page 53, is that the responses of individuals lead to mutual and positive reinforcement. We shall first describe a study demonstrating how cooperative behavior develops in the absence of communication, and—as a matter of fact—in the absence of awareness on the part of the individuals that they are indeed cooperating with one another.

Sidowski, Wyckoff, and Tabory (1956) studied pairs of subjects engaged in a learning task requiring joint responses. In each pair, the subjects were isolated from each other and ignorant of each other's existence. The subjects were brought into separate rooms. Each room (A and B) was equipped with two switches, a digital counter, and a source of electric shock. Electrodes were attached to two fingers of each subject's left hand. The switches in Room A controlled positive and negative reinforcement for the subject in Room B, and the switches in Room B controlled these reinforcing events for the subject in Room A. Positive reinforcement was "scoring points" on the digital counter, while negative reinforcement was electric shock, delivered through the electrodes. Thus, when the subject in Room A pressed his right-hand switch, the counter in Room B registered one point in favor of the subject in Room B. If the subject in Room A pressed the left-hand switch, the subject in Room B received an electric shock. Similarly, the subject in Room B had control over the counter scores and the number of shocks given to the subject in Room A. Neither had direct control over his own point score or shock; and, as we said before, each subject thought that, besides the experimenter, he was the only person in the situation.

Ostensibly, the task was to amass as many points as possible by operating the two switches. The subject could press either switch at any time, although not both of them simultaneously. He could also press the switches as long and often as he wanted to. The entire experimental session continued 25 minutes.

Of course, the main interest of the experimenters was to determine whether cooperative behavior would develop in this situation. And the subjects pressed the switch that accumulated points for their unseen and unknown partners nearly twice as often as the "punishing" switch. The average number of rewarding responses over the 25-minute period was 1037.7, and of the punishing responses 558.9. Naturally, in the beginning there were as many rewarding as punishing responses. But during the second minute of the experimental session a clear preference for the rewarding responses emerged.

Consider the behavior of the subject in this experiment in the light of the paradigm of cooperation on page 53. Throughout the experimental session each subject has only two response alternatives: He can activate his left-hand switch or his right-hand switch. And since each subject can respond as he wants to, the first *joint* response of the two subjects is a matter of chance. There are four distinct possibilities for the first joint response of the two subjects:

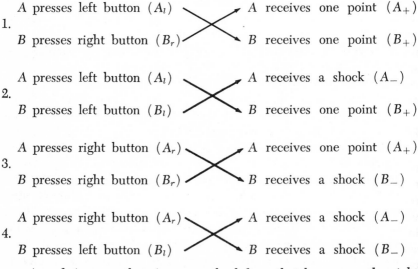

1.
A presses left button (A_l) — A receives one point (A_+)
B presses right button (B_r) — B receives one point (B_+)

2.
A presses left button (A_l) — A receives a shock (A_-)
B presses left button (B_l) — B receives one point (B_+)

3.
A presses right button (A_r) — A receives one point (A_+)
B presses right button (B_r) — B receives a shock (B_-)

4.
A presses right button (A_r) — A receives a shock (A_-)
B presses left button (B_l) — B receives a shock (B_-)

A_l and A_r mean that A presses the left or that he presses the right button respectively; B_l and B_r mean that B presses the left or the right button; A_+ and A_- mean that A receives a point or a shock; and B_+ and B_- mean that B receives a point or a shock; and the arrows mean "leads to."

The following analysis is from Kelley, Thibaut, Radloff, and Mundy (1962), and it is based on a theory of interpersonal behavior recently elaborated by Thibaut and Kelley (1959), which the student will find of considerable interest.

Let us assume that the tendency to continue with the same response is strengthened when the response is followed by reward (scoring a point), and that it is weakened when it is followed by punishment (receiving shock). We would, therefore, expect the following four patterns of joint responses to emerge:

SUCCESSIVE JOINT RESPONSES OF A AND B

1	2	3	4	...

1.
A_l ✕ A_+ ⟶ A_l ✕ A_+ ⟶ A_l ✕ A_+ ⟶ A_l ✕ A_+ ...
B_r ✕ B_+ ⟶ B_r ✕ B_+ ⟶ B_r ✕ B_+ ⟶ B_r ✕ B_+

2.
A_l ✕ A_- ⟶ A_r ✕ A_- ⟶ A_l ✕ A_+ ⟶ A_l ✕ A_+ ...
B_l ✕ B_+ ⟶ B_l ✕ B_- ⟶ B_r ✕ B_+ ⟶ B_r ✕ B_+

3.
A_r ✕ A_+ ⟶ A_r ✕ A_- ⟶ A_l ✕ A_+ ⟶ A_l ✕ A_+ ...
B_r ✕ B_- ⟶ B_l ✕ B_- ⟶ B_r ✕ B_+ ⟶ B_r ✕ B_+

4.
A_r ✕ A_- ⟶ A_l ✕ A_+ ⟶ A_l ✕ A_+ ⟶ A_l ✕ A_+ ...
B_l ✕ B_- ⟶ B_r ✕ B_+ ⟶ B_r ✕ B_+ ⟶ B_r ✕ B_+

In the diagram, when A and B begin with two mutually rewarding responses (alternative 1), cooperation is likely to continue. If, in the beginning, one subject rewards the other and the other reciprocates with punishment (alternatives 2 and 3), cooperative behavior will not develop until the third joint response. When the subjects begin the session by punishing each other (alternative 4), cooperation will develop on the second joint response.

Although the above diagram assumes that the rule "point, stay—shock, change" applies without exception, there are, of course, individual variations, but the above analysis leads us to expect cooperative behavior to develop rather rapidly—and the findings of Sidowski, Wyckoff, and Tabory (1956) confirm this expectation. Figure 13 shows that cooperation can develop in a matter of minutes. However, the efficiency of the cooperative process was not at the highest possible level. Even toward the end of the experimental session the two individuals "punished" each

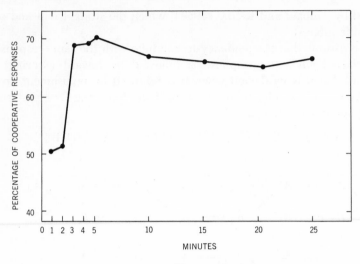

Figure 13

The emergence of cooperative behavior in the absence of communication. (Redrawn from data reported by Sidowski, Wyckoff, and Tabory, 1956.)

other on the average over 30 percent of the time. No doubt the efficiency of the cooperative process, and the speed with which the process can develop, depend on the subjects' awareness of their mutual response-reinforcement contingency, as well as on their opportunity and ability to coordinate their joint responses by communication.

But under some conditions individuals, although interdependent in reinforcement, are quite unlikely to cooperate. Consider a situation identical to the one in the Sidowski-Wyckoff-Tabory experiment, except that each of the two subjects has a fixed interval of time in which he may respond, and that these intervals alternate between the two subjects. During the first interval A must make a choice among the buttons and press one; during the second, B must make one of the two responses; during the third interval A must respond again; and so on. The patterns shown on p. 71 develop.

Among these four patterns, either cooperative behavior emerges during the first time interval and continues from then on (pattern 1) or it never develops (patterns 2, 3, and 4). (The "never" in this hypothesis holds only if the "point, stay—shock, change" rule applies absolutely; and, of course, there are exceptions.)

To examine this hypothesis Kelley, Thibaut, Radloff, and Mundy (1962) carried out an experiment quite similar to the one originally performed by Sidowski, Wyckoff, and Tabory. Two groups of subjects were

SUCCESSIVE TIME INTERVALS

	1	2	3	4	5 . . .

1.
$A_l \quad A_+ \rightarrow A_l \quad A_+ \rightarrow A_l \quad A_+ \rightarrow A_l \quad A_+ \rightarrow A_l \quad A_+ \; \cdots$
$B_+ \rightarrow B_r \quad B_+ \rightarrow B_r \quad B_+ \rightarrow B_r \quad B_+ \rightarrow B_r \quad B_+ \rightarrow B_r$

2.
$A_l \quad A_- \rightarrow A_r \quad A_+ \rightarrow A_r \quad A_- \rightarrow A_l \quad A_- \rightarrow A_r \quad A_+ \; \cdots$
$B_+ \rightarrow B_l \quad B_- \rightarrow B_r \quad B_- \rightarrow B_l \quad B_+ \rightarrow B_l \quad B_- \rightarrow B_r$

3.
$A_r \quad A_+ \rightarrow A_r \quad A_- \rightarrow A_l \quad A_- \rightarrow A_r \quad A_+ \rightarrow A_r \quad A_- \; \cdots$
$B_- \rightarrow B_r \quad B_- \rightarrow B_l \quad B_+ \rightarrow B_l \quad B_- \rightarrow B_r \quad B_- \rightarrow B_l$

4.
$A_r \quad A_- \rightarrow A_l \quad A_- \rightarrow A_r \quad A_+ \rightarrow A_r \quad A_- \rightarrow A_l \quad A_- \; \cdots$
$B_- \rightarrow B_l \quad B_+ \rightarrow B_l \quad B_- \rightarrow B_r \quad B_- \rightarrow B_l \quad B_+ \rightarrow B_l$

treated like those in the Sidowski-Wyckoff-Tabory experiment, while two other groups were explicitly told about the presence of the other subject, and about the manner in which he completely controlled their scores. In one of the first and in one of the second set of groups the subjects were given an opportunity to respond simultaneously, and in the other two sets the opportunity to respond alternated between the subjects. These four groups may be called Simultaneous Naive, Simultaneous Informed, Alternating Naive, and Alternating Informed. Each of these groups of subject pairs received over 100 trials in blocks of 35. The results in Figure 14 show, first of all, that the proportion of cooperative responses in the Simultaneous Naive group rose quite slowly; and if the experiment had not stopped at the 175th trial, cooperation would in all probability have reached a higher level than in the Sidowski-Wyckoff-Tabory experiment. The graph also shows that when the subjects were aware that their reinforcement was mutually interdependent (dashed curves), cooperative behavior reached a higher level than when they worked in ignorance of each other—a finding quite consistent with what we would expect intuitively. However, also consistently with expectations that were not intuitive but arrived at by means of detailed analysis, the subjects responding simultaneously (open circles) showed substantially more cooperative behavior than subjects in the alternating groups (closed circles), regardless of whether they were aware or unaware of each other's presence. The experimenters' prediction that cooperation

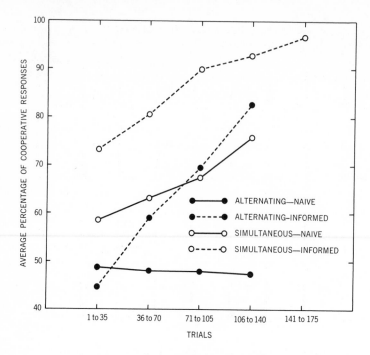

Figure 14

Cooperative behavior of naive and informed subjects under alternating and simultaneous response conditions. (Drawn from data reported by Kelley, Thibaut, Radloff, and Mundy, 1962.)

would not develop among Alternating Naive subjects was fully confirmed. Throughout the experimental session, these subjects issued equal amounts of positive and negative reinforcement to their partners.

THE CHOICE TO COOPERATE OR TO COMPETE

The experiments by Sidowski, Wyckoff, and Tabory and by Kelley, Thibaut, Radloff, and Mundy deal with the simplest case of cooperative behavior. In both studies the subjects' responses controlled reinforcement for their partners; the subjects could not control their own reinforcement. Normally, however, in everyday cooperation situations, and in the paradigm on page 53, cooperation and competition are assumed to involve responses that have reinforcing consequences not only for one's partner but for oneself as well. Thus, we think of cooperation when what *A* does is simultaneously beneficial to him as well as to *B*, and when what *B* does is simultaneously beneficial to both. On the contrary, we think of competition when what *A* does is to his own benefit but to *B*'s disadvantage, and when what B does is in turn to his own benefit but to A's disadvantage. If A's responses have the same reinforcement consequences for him and for his partner, and if the same is true for B's responses, then cooperative behavior will readily develop, for it is to each individual's advantage to choose the positively reinforcing alternative. Translating the Miller-Banks-Ogawa experiments (1962, 1963) reviewed earlier into present terms, each monkey had a "choice" of responding or not responding. The subject with the stimulus (light) had a "choice" between overtly responding to it or not and thus communicating its onset to his partner. The subject with the response bar, on the other hand, could either press it or ignore it. But it was to each animal's advantage to respond positively. The benefit of one animal led to an equal benefit of the other (both avoided an unpleasant shock), and the harm to one coincided with an equal harm to the other. The situation in the Miller-Banks-Ogawa experiments may be represented by Table 2.

Table 2

	PRESS	NOT PRESS	SIGNAL	NOT SIGNAL
	A's RESPONSE		B's RESPONSE	
A's reinforcement	+	−	+	−
B's reinforcement	+	−	+	−

To avoid shock, the monkeys had to choose the appropriate response *and coordinate responding:* they could avoid shock only if A pressed the bar at the appropriate time (within 6 seconds after the light went on), and A could respond at the appropriate time only if B signaled to him. Of course, if A made a bar-pressing response every few seconds, he would by chance alone avoid shock for himself as well as for his partner. He could then get along without B's contribution, and B would in that case become A's parasite.

The effort to coordinate responses may at times hinder or delay cooperation. Moreover, one subject may be tempted to follow a selfish "strategy" at the expense of his partner. An alternative equally beneficial to both partners may provide less total benefit than another one that gives greater benefit to one and a smaller benefit (or even harm) to the other. In Table 3 A and B can each choose between two responses—let us say, "left" and "right." Each partner's outcome (in cents) depends on their joint responses. The first amount in each cell of the matrix represent's A's outcome, and the second B's outcome. If A chooses "left" he can win either 3¢ or 5¢, and if he chooses "right" he can win either 0¢ or 1¢, depending on what B chooses. A wins 3¢ if he chooses "left" and if B also chooses left. But A can win 5¢ if he chooses "left" and B chooses "right."

Table 3

B's RESPONSES

		LEFT	RIGHT
A's RESPONSES	LEFT	3¢, 3¢	5¢, 0¢
	RIGHT	0¢, 5¢	1¢, 1¢

Similarly, if B chooses left, he can win either 3¢ or 5¢, depending on whether A chooses "left" or "right" respectively, or he can win nothing or a penny when A chooses "right."

Clearly, A's best strategy is to choose "left." The *least* he can win is 3¢. If he chose "right," his *maximum* win would only be 1¢. From B's point of view it is also best to choose "left," and for exactly the same reason. No doubt in the situation shown in Table 3 both partners would end up choosing "left."

But consider Table 4. Choosing "left" can get A either 3¢ or nothing. Choosing "right" promises either a nickel or a penny. The second alternative is clearly preferable. Choosing "left" can bring B either 3¢ or nothing—while he can win as much as a nickel, and at least a penny, if he

Table 4

B's RESPONSES

		LEFT	RIGHT
A's RESPONSES	LEFT	3¢, 3¢	0¢, 5¢
	RIGHT	5¢, 0¢	1¢, 1¢

chooses "right." Thus for B "right" also represents the best strategy. But if A and B both choose "right," each will gain only a penny; note that if they each choose left they can win three times as much. If A and B are to make such choices repeatedly and if the relationship is to continue, they would definitely benefit in the long run from choosing "left." If both participants are to reap greater benefit from their joint responses, each must sacrifice the prospect of a higher but immediate and somewhat uncertain gain, for the security of a lesser but a more stable one. Each partner must withstand the temptation of selfish motives.

Several experiments have used the situations like those above—for instance, Scodel, Minas, Ratoosh, and Lipetz, 1959. In a typical experiment two subjects, aware of each other's presence and seated in separate rooms, are told that they will "have a chance to make some money in this situation." On a table in front of the subject are two buttons for signaling his choices and two lights to indicate his partner's choices. The consequences of the payoffs are carefully explained, and the subjects know what they and their partners will receive as a result of each of the four possible joint choices. The choices are made repeatedly, but the instructions tend not to present the task as a game, and the experimenter carefully avoids words like "play," "win," and "lose," in order not to foster inadvertently either cooperation or competition among the subjects. A response that benefits the partner and promises a small long-run payoff, at a sacrifice of some self-interest, is *cooperative*. (For example, a "left" response in Table 4.) A response that promises a larger temporary payoff, at a definite disadvantage to the partner, is called *noncooperative*. (For example, a "right" response in Table 4.)

In experiments of this sort the proportion of cooperative choices made by subjects seldom exceeds 50 percent—even when the situation promises an immediate high reward for cooperation. Table 5 shows some of the different payoff schemes used by Minas, Scodel, Marlowe, and Rawson (1960). The smallest amount of cooperation was found in Situation II, in which the possible gain of the noncooperative choice—that is, $(5¢ + 1¢)/2$—was twice the gain of a cooperative choice—that is, $(3¢ + 0¢)/2$. When the possible gain of the noncooperative choice was half again as large as that following the cooperative choice, as in Situation I, only a negligible increase in cooperativeness occurred. Even when the immediate gain of cooperation was greater than the immediate gain of noncooperation (Situations III, IV, V, and VI), the amount of cooperation was not terribly impressive. In Situation IV, for instance, the subject choosing "left" could make either as much as 6¢ but not less than 4¢. Choosing "right" could get him 7¢ (a penny more than the maximum of the "left" choice), but it could also lead to a loss of 3¢. Clearly, under these conditions, in the short run and in the long run, it was to his advantage to make cooperative choices. However, subjects in this situation made on the average only 53 percent cooperative choices. Apparently, they were more concerned with making more (or losing less) money than their partners than in making some money at all. Also, fewer cooperative responses were made during the first half of the experimental session than during the second half.

Why don't we find in these situations a stronger tendency to cooperate? Does cooperation here depend on trust? For instance in Table 6, *B* may agree to cooperate and consistently choose "left," guaranteeing $1,000 to *A* when the latter also chooses "left." But *A* may very well choose "right" on some occasions, making ten times as much money and

Table 5

Percent of cooperative responses in various payoff situations. (From Minas, Scodel, Marlowe, and Rawson, 1960.)

SITUATION I

B'S RESPONSES

		LEFT	RIGHT
A's RESPONSES	LEFT	8¢, 8¢	1¢, 10¢
	RIGHT	10¢, 1¢	2¢, 2¢

38% cooperative behavior

SITUATION II

B'S RESPONSES

		LEFT	RIGHT
A's RESPONSES	LEFT	3¢, 3¢	0¢, 5¢
	RIGHT	5¢, 0¢	1¢, 1¢

36% cooperative behavior

SITUATION III

B'S RESPONSES

		LEFT	RIGHT
A's RESPONSES	LEFT	6¢, 6¢	4¢, 7¢
	RIGHT	7¢, 4¢	−1¢, −1¢

50% cooperative behavior

SITUATION IV

B'S RESPONSES

		LEFT	RIGHT
A's RESPONSES	LEFT	6¢, 6¢	4¢, 7¢
	RIGHT	7¢, 4¢	−3¢, −3¢

53% cooperative behavior

SITUATION V

B'S RESPONSES

		LEFT	RIGHT
A's RESPONSES	LEFT	3¢, 3¢	1¢, 3¢
	RIGHT	3¢, 1¢	0¢, 0¢

48% cooperative behavior

SITUATION VI

B'S RESPONSES

		LEFT	RIGHT
A's RESPONSES	LEFT	4¢, 4¢	1¢, 3¢
	RIGHT	3¢, 1¢	0¢, 0¢

53% cooperative behavior

simultaneously causing B a loss of $10,000. Before B will settle on consistently choosing left he must trust that A will do the same. But what actually happens? Using the payoff scheme from Situation II, Minas, Scodel, Marlowe, and Rawson (1960) have simulated the responses of B. Even when the subjects thought that their partners cooperated 100 percent of the time, they themselves cooperated only 38 percent of the time! Bixenstine, Potash, and Wilson (1963)—also using Situation II—simulated that B cooperated either 83 or 17 percent of the time. Their subjects cooperated only 33 and 30 percent of the time respectively.

Table 6

B's RESPONSES

		LEFT		RIGHT	
A's RESPONSES	LEFT	+$ 1,000	+$ 1,000	−$10,000	+$10,000
	RIGHT	+$10,000	−$10,000	−$10,000	−$10,000

However, Bixenstine and Wilson (1963) found some change in the cooperative behavior of subjects when the simulated responses of the "partner" changed. Subjects in a situation similar to the previous one interacted with a simulated partner over a series of 200 trials. In one group the series consisted of forty trials during which the simulated partner cooperated 95 percent of the time, twenty trials 50 percent of the time, eighty trials 5 percent, twenty trials 50 percent, and again forty trials 95 percent, in that order. In another group the order was inverted, the series now consisting of 40 trials at 5 percent, and so on. The results in Figure 15 show that when cooperativeness of the simulated partner increased, the subject's cooperative choices increased. But even when the simulated responses were at 95 percent of cooperation, the subjects did not fully reciprocate, limiting their own cooperative choices to 50 percent.

We will discover the reason for the lack of cooperation if we look at the payoff scheme, sometimes called the payoff matrix, used in the Bixenstine experiments (Table 7). We see that if B (the simulated partner) chooses "left" 83 percent of the time, and if the game is played

Table 7

B's (SIMULATED) RESPONSES

		LEFT	RIGHT
A's SUBJECT RESPONSES	LEFT	3¢, 3¢	0¢, 5¢
	RIGHT	5¢, 0¢	1¢, 1¢

for 100 trials, A can make $2.49 (83 × 3¢ + 17 × 0¢) when he consistently chooses "left," but he can make $4.32 (83 × 5¢ + 17 × 1¢) when he persists in choosing "right." Thus, it is to A's own advantage not to cooperate once he knows that B will almost always choose "left." If B is simulated to choose the noncooperative option 83 percent of the time, A will make $1.68 when he chooses "right" on all 100 trials but only $.41 when he chooses "left." Again it is to A's advantage not to cooperate. With the simulated partner cooperating 83 percent of the time, and with

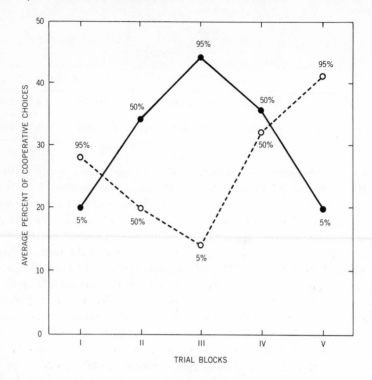

Figure 15

Proportion of cooperative choices as a function of partner's cooperativeness. Values on the graph indicate percent of cooperative choices made by the simulated partner. (Redrawn from data reported by Bixenstine and Wilson, 1963, with the permission of the authors and the publisher.)

A consistently failing to cooperate, A sees B winning only $.17, while he himself cashes in $4.32. The welfare of one's partner is apparently of little significance to the individual, according to the findings of Bixenstine, Potash, and Wilson (1963).

In everyday life most competitive and cooperative relationships are highly conventionalized, institutionalized, and organized; and they seldom allow us to choose between cooperating and competing. If we join a sports team, we either play for its benefit, or we do not play at all. When a violinist joins an orchestra, he may at first compete for the chair he is allowed to challenge; but once a decision has been made, he must accept the verdict and begin contributing what is asked of him. And two competing business enterprises seldom merge out of sheer desire to cooperate with one another.

CONFLICT, COMPETITION, AND THEIR CONSEQUENCES

We said in the introduction to Part I that *conflict* between individuals is a special case of competition. To discover what sort of special case it is, Warren and Maroney (1958) studied for over six months the behavior of three groups of rhesus monkeys—each group composed of three females and three males. In each group, each animal was paired repeatedly with every other animal in a situation requiring them to compete for food. The experimenter placed in the test cage with two monkeys a food morsel large enough for only one animal and observed which of the two secured it. During all tests the experimenter observed the general level of the animals' activity, their aggressiveness toward each other, and the amount of time each took to secure the food for himself. Figure 16 shows the average percentage of success in competition for food in a series of six tests spread out over six months. (For economy, the figure concerns only one of the three groups.) Each point on these curves represents the percentage success for a given animal averaged over all of his confrontations with all other animals, one at a time, and on repeated occasions. We note from Figure 16 that the initially successful animals (4 and 18, for instance) tended to become even more successful, and the initially unsuccessful monkeys (12 and 14) became more unsuccessful. In other words, *a clear dominance hierarchy developed*, and it seemed to maintain a great deal of stability.

What accounted for an animal's rank in the hierarchy? Warren and Maroney found that ranking was not a result of sex, weight, or overall activity level. One factor closely related to the animal's dominance position was his aggressiveness during the early stages of testing. Table 8 shows for the same group as in Figure 16 that there is a strong associa-

Table 8

Incidence of aggressive behavior in the early and late test series (recomputed). (From Warren and Maroney, 1958.)

		EARLY TEST SERIES		LATE TEST SERIES	
ANIMAL NO.	SEX	BIT OR STRUCK OTHERS	WAS BITTEN OR STRUCK	BIT OR STRUCK OTHERS	WAS BITTEN OR STRUCK
4	♀	6	10	3	0
9	♀	10	22	3	1
12	♀	0	10	0	1
13	♂	21	11	died	
14	♂	2	67	0	3
18	♂	82	1	2	3

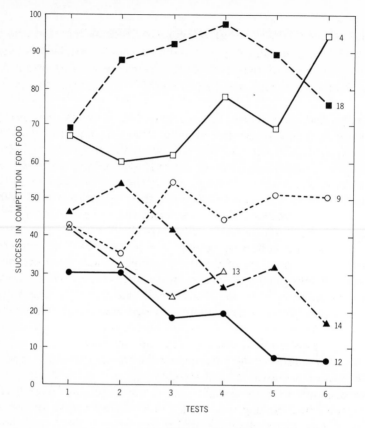

Figure 16

Percent success in competition for food among six rhesus monkeys. (Redrawn from Warren and Maroney, Journal of Social Psychology, *1958, 48, 223–233.)*

tion between aggressiveness and the dominance status of the animal. For all three groups, the correlation between early aggressiveness and dominance was +.77. Also clear from these data is the fact that the animals showed ten times more aggressiveness toward the end of testing than they did at the beginning.

Let us now return to the original problem. The difference between conflict and competition, we maintain, corresponds to the difference between the early and late stages of the development of the dominance hierarchy in the experiment we have just described. Note that there is no difference between the early and late stages in terms of reinforcement interdependence. If animal No. 18 gets a raisin, No. 12 cannot have it;

and this is equally true of the late stage of testing as it is of the early one. There is, however, a difference in the instrumental behavior which establishes the animals' priorities with respect to food privileges. The basic difference between the two periods seems to be that there are practically no restrictions on the methods the animals use in obtaining food during the early stages, but that competition for food is *conventionalized* during the later stages—as if there were precedence rules for food, and a prohibition against using aggression to get food. We can therefore say that when conventional controls over instrumental behavior are lacking in a competitive situation, conflict exists. The racial crisis in the United States represents a conflict in which past conventional controls over racial competition for economic, social, and political privileges are disintegrating. The resolution of this conflict hopefully rests with legislating a new set of conventional controls to govern competition equitably.

This definition of interindividual or intergroup conflict directs our research efforts not only toward the causes of conflict, but also toward the problem of how conflict can be turned into competition. We can phrase our research questions primarily to discover how conflicts occur and how to resolve them. Under what conditions will a set of rules develop to control instrumental behavior of conflicting parties? Under what conditions will such a development take place rapidly? What factors inhibit the development of conventional controls? What aspects of instrumental conflict behavior are first to fall under conventional controls? These questions are of great social significance today when the world is beset by a host of intergroup conflicts. For if today's major conflicts cannot be turned into institutionalized competition, they can only lead to the elimination of the antagonists.

PART THREE

GROUP
PROCESSES

Rousseau said that man's weakness lies in the excess of his wants over his ability to satisfy them. No human infant would survive if he had to depend entirely upon himself to satisfy his basic biological needs, and no pharaoh would have his pyramid if he had to depend entirely on his own ingenuity and effort. Yet men together can gratify their own wants and the wants of others as well; the family and other human associations have helped man to survive and flourish.

Men pay a price for these associations. Two men sawing a log will benefit from the cut log, but they must also surrender to each other a fraction of their individuality, uniqueness, and independence. They must pull in rhythm, at the same pace, and in the same plane; they must reach some degree of *uniformity*. This amounts to saying that they must surrender their idiosyncrasies to each other.

Yet the two cutters must also become *differentiated* from one another in many respects. They must choose different ends of the saw. Also, they cannot pull their ends at the same time, but must alternate and coordinate their actions with one another. Thus, whether the social process emerges into uniformity or into differentiation, the individual's choices are limited and he must sacrifice some of his uniqueness.

The last two chapters of this book are devoted to the products and costs of social interaction. Chapter 8 will be concerned with the "cost" of social interaction: the natures and processes of social uniformities and social differentiation. Chapter 9 will examine the benefits that derive from the group: how a number of individuals together can produce more than each could produce by himself.

SOCIAL UNIFORMITIES AND
SOCIAL DIFFERENTIATION

8

SOCIAL UNIFORMITIES

As mentioned in Chapter 3, Chen (1937) observed dramatic increases in performance when ants who had been working alone began to work together. But Chen discovered even more striking evidence about the social sensitivity of these insects when he paired slow or fast working ants with ants known to be mediocre at nest building. Chen placed two ants together at a time in a bottle and recorded how long it took them to begin working, and the number of pellets each carried from the interior of the nest to the outside in 5-minute intervals. Figure 17 leaves little doubt that the productivity of the test subject (M) is influenced adversely by the presence of a slow companion (S) and enhanced by the presence of a rapid one (R). There seems to be a tendency on the part of the test ant to gauge its behavior in terms of the behavior of its companion. But we should not draw our conclusions prematurely. The two tests were performed on two different occasions, and M's behavior could have been influenced by factors other than the presence of R or S. Besides, Figure 17 shows data for one animal only. The conclusion is strengthened by data shown in Table 5 which records similar experimental results for ten workers, previously known to be of mediocre caliber.

Chen's findings are truly remarkable. First, there are pronounced variations among the various pairs of ants. Some ants began nest building after one hour and 20 minutes (M_1:R, for instance), others after hardly 1½ minutes (M_7:S). (Remember from Chapter 3 that the average latency of ants working alone was around three hours, thus, the social facilitation effect is also present here.) But, secondly, except for the M_1:R pair, the two ants of each pair began working at nearly the same time—meaning that the mediocre ants adjusted their behavior to that of their partners, whether their partners were rapid or slow. For instance, subject M_2 waited nearly one hour before beginning to work on his nest when paired with a slow partner, but only 7.28 minutes when placed with a rapid one. In this experiment, on the average the ants began working seven times quicker when they were paired with a rapid co-worker than when they were paired with a slow one. Also, the average absolute difference in the latencies between the members of a given pair (shown in columns 6 and 8 of Table 9) was considerably smaller than the average difference

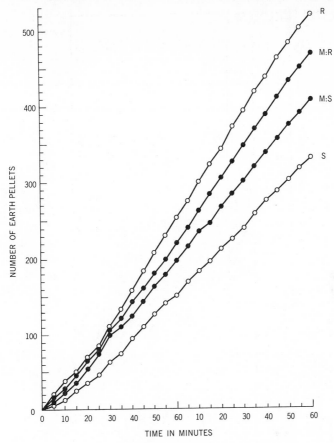

Figure 17

*Nest building of an ant paired with a slow co-
worker (M:S) and with a rapid co-worker (M:R).
The performance of the slow and rapid workers
(S and R) is also shown. (From Chen, 1937 with permission of publisher.)*

in the behavior of the same ant when paired with rapid and slow partners
(column 7)!

ACHIEVING SOCIAL UNIFORMITY

All animals show various forms of uniformities—behavioral and
morphological. All human beings have the same number of vertebra; all
Indians have black hair; all cats meow; and all members of *Camarhyn-
chus pallidus* (finch) of the Galapagos Islands apparently carry a cactus
spine in their beaks to pick out insects from tree bark (Dobzhansky,
1955). All morphological and many behavioral uniformities are geneti-

Table 9

Latency of the nest-building response of ten ants with mediocre latency, working with slow and rapid partners. (From Chen, 1937, with permission of publisher.)

TEST ANT NO.	LATENCY IN MINUTES				ABSOLUTE DIFFERENCES IN LATENCIES		
	WORKING WITH A SLOW (S) PARTNER		WORKING WITH A RAPID (R) PARTNER				
	LATENCY OF S S	LATENCY OF M $M:S$	LATENCY OF M $M:R$	LATENCY OF R R	$\|M:S - S\|$	$\|M:S - M:R\|$	$\|M:R - R\|$
(1)	(2)	(3)	(4)	(5)	(6)	(7)	(8)
M_1	79.75	80.08	2.23	77.15	.33	77.85	74.92
M_2	61.17	56.30	7.28	7.00	4.87	49.02	.28
M_3	58.72	58.48	10.47	12.42	.24	48.01	1.95
M_4	17.57	14.93	1.45	1.32	2.64	13.48	.07
M_5	8.05	8.17	.85	.87	.12	7.32	.02
M_6	7.80	7.88	4.62	4.67	.08	3.26	.05
M_7	7.63	7.28	.87	.88	.35	6.41	.01
M_8	6.17	1.08	.97	.92	5.09	.11	.05
M_9	5.28	4.62	2.18	1.85	.66	2.44	.33
M_{10}	3.03	2.77	1.93	1.05	.26	.84	.88
Average	25.52	24.16	3.28	10.81	4.64	20.88	7.86

cally determined. But some behavioral uniformities are the consequence of social interaction. The uniformity in the latencies of the ants' nest building was socially determined because it arose as a consequence of a reciprocal influence process. And perhaps the use of the cactus spine by the Galapagos finch is also a socially determined uniformity, for the parents might have taught the young finches to use the spines. Unlike genetically determined uniformities which need no maintenance (such as number of vertebra in human beings), social uniformities arise as a consequence of a social process, and are maintained by a social process as well. The processes previously examined—coaction, imitation, vicarious learning, communication, cooperation, and even conflict—are mainly sources of social uniformity. Conformity, however, is a process that maintains social uniformities.

All animals, including man, are extremely sensitive to social uniformities. We have seen how pressures toward uniformity may determine the flow and the rate of communication in informal social groups (p. 58ff). We have also touched upon a curious finding reported by Floyd Allport which he obtained in his studies of coaction (p. 21), to which we now return. Allport (1924) found that individuals who had been working alone and began to work in the presence of others increased their performance for tasks involving past skills and decreased for tasks involving learning or problem solving. On judgment tasks, however, the only effect was a reduction in the tendency to make extreme judgments. When the judgments of the pleasantness of odors and of the heaviness of weights were made in groups, a considerably smaller number of extreme ratings were found. Unpleasant odors were rated less unpleasant in groups and pleasant odors less pleasant. Heavy weights were judged somewhat lighter in groups and light weights somewhat heavier. Allport explained the experimental finding:

. . . In the writer's opinion it is the result of an attitude of submission which we assume, often unconsciously, in the presence of a group. Where all are engaged upon the same sort of task this submission takes the character of *conforming* to the manner in which the other members are reacting. More specifically, upon approaching the extreme of the series, the question arises in the subject's consciousness, "How extreme shall I make this judgment?" He feels that he is more likely to be at odds with the judgment of his associates if he goes too far than if not quite extreme enough. Hence he errs upon the side of moderation . . . There is a basic human tendency to temper one's opinions and conduct by deference to the opinions and conduct of others. Early training and social contact have bred in us the avoidance of extremes of all sorts, whether in clothing, of manners, or of belief (pp. 277–278).[1]

[1] Floyd H. Allport, *Social Psychology* (Boston: Houghton Mifflin Co., 1924), pp. 277–278. Reprinted with permission of author and publisher.

Allport's subjects *wrote* down their judgments, so that even in the coacting situation none knew the others' responses. Yet apparently the sheer presence of others was sufficient to produce the convergence effect.

The studies on conformity reviewed in Chapter 4 shed some light on the vulnerability of the solitary individual to the opinions of others. When an individual is confronted with a contrary uniform group opinion, he generally yields to the majority—even when physical evidence clearly contradicts the majority opinion. How strong and permanent are such effects? How will a group of naive individuals who must make judgments of an ambiguous event behave? Let us examine two studies which deal with these questions in the laboratory, both of which used the *autokinetic effect*. This effect is obtained when a person in darkness observes a stationary point of light that appears to move. (See Weintraub and Walker, 1966.) The effect is often obtained even when the person is told that the light is perfectly stationary. However, the illusion is particularly pronounced when the subject is unaware of the distance between himself and the light, when the field is completely darkened, and when he believes that the light might move.

Sherif (1936) successfully utilized the autokinetic effect to study the formation and stability of uniformities. He collected judgments about the alleged movement of a stationary light from individuals and two- and three-person groups. The subjects were told that when the room was completely dark a pinpoint of light would appear in front of them and, shortly afterward, begin to move. Their task was to signal when the light began to move, and to announce aloud how many inches it moved each time.

Two conditions were examined, each involving four daily sessions, and each requiring the subject to make 100 judgments. In one condition, the subjects spent the first session in isolation and the last three in groups of two or three people. In the other condition, the subjects spent three consecutive sessions in groups and the final session alone. From this study, three clear findings emerge: (1) solitary judgments that precede group judgments diverge from one another, showing normal interindividual variability; (2) when group judgments follow solitary judgments, interindividual variability disappears and the judgments tend to converge with one another; and (3) individual judgments that follow group judgments fail to show interindividual variability. In brief, the group situation results in uniformity among the individual judgments, and the individual maintains the judgment he first made in the group situation, even when he is no longer with his group.

Sherif's findings, like Asch's (1952), may give support to the once popular idea that in group situations the individual *completely* surrenders his independence and integrity. Gustave Le Bon (1896), an early social psychologist who took his examples from revolutionary crowds, argued that in group situations a person's uniqueness and individuality wilt, his good sense and judgment leave him, and he becomes an uncivilized animal capable of most heinous actions.

But can a group, society, or culture justify any action, make any belief seem true, and *any* custom right? Probably not. True, infanticide still occurs, and some still believe that the number thirteen can bring bad luck. But slavery no longer exists, and we no longer use cupping glasses. Our beliefs have changed in the last century toward a greater correspondence with objective reality, and our customs toward a greater respect for individual life and worth. Lest we take the results of Asch and Sherif as proof of the weakness of the individual *vis-à-vis* his society and culture, we must consider a recent experiment.

The finding of Jacobs and Campbell (1961) strongly suggest that man is not completely culture-bound. Jacobs and Campbell attempted to create experimentally the common belief that the light in an autokinetic situation moves 15 or 16 inches; they also attempted to observe the stability of this belief over several laboratory "generations." Sherif examined the development of a group "norm" and observed its influence upon the group members, but he dealt with only one generation. One of the important properties of social conventions is that they are transmitted, by various forms of learning, from one generation to the next. The Jacobs and Campbell experimental session began with two confederates and one subject. (Note that an individual experiencing the autokinetic effect alone sees the light "move" about 4 inches.) On the first trial the two confederates, as previously instructed, announced one after another that the light had moved 15 or 16 inches, and then the subject announced his judgment. This procedure was repeated thirty times. Then one of the confederates was replaced by a new naive subject. The subject there previously now responded second, while the new subject announced his judgment last. Again thirty trials were conducted, with the remaining confederate varying his judgments around 16 inches. After the second block of thirty trials, the second confederate was replaced by another naive subject. Following the third trial block, the first subject introduced to the group was replaced by a new naive one. Following the fourth trial block, the second subject was replaced, and so on for ten consecutive trial blocks. Thus each subject served for three consecutive trial blocks, carrying on the "tradition" of his experimental culture, which he inherited from the confederates or from his ancestor subjects. In a control condition the same process of replacement occurred, but without confederates. Figure 18 compares the experimental and control conditions. When no

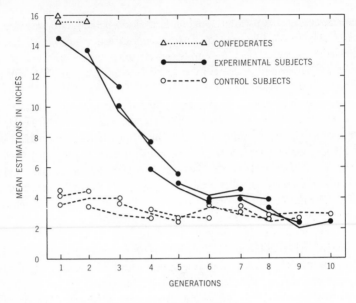

Figure 18

The transmission of an arbitrary norm in a three-person group. (Redrawn from Jacobs and Campbell, 1961, with permission of author and publisher.)

arbitrary norm was imposed on the group (control), the judgments fluctuated around 3 to 4 inches—the same results that Sherif obtained in his study. In the control condition, judgments of successive replacements did not differ very much from one another. In the experimental group the two confederates at the beginning pushed the group norm up to 14 or 15 inches. But as the confederates began to be replaced by naive subjects, and old subjects were replaced by newcomers, the average estimate dropped. By the sixth trial block—that is, by the time the fourth subject was replaced—there was no difference between the group whose original "tradition" was 15 or 16 inches and the group whose original "tradition" fluctuated between 3 and 4 inches. Jacobs and Campbell concluded that

> . . . the outcome may well warn us against the assumption that a purely arbitrary cultural norm could be perpetuated indefinitely *without other sources of support.*[2] Even if people weigh the opinions of their elders many times that of their own direct observations, the collective effect of their own observations probably soon erodes a *functionless* arbitrary belief. Where we observed tenacious bizarre cultural belief we must look to more

[2] Italics mine.

than mere tradition, suggestibility, or conformity, to explain its retention (p. 657).[3]

Uniformities, when perpetuated over generations by means of social learning, are the essence of culture. Can animals perpetuate uniformities, and do they have cultures? Although the behavior of animals can be influenced systematically by the behavior of other members of the species, it is generally doubted that *any* animal species has what we would call a culture. However, a few dissenting voices have been heard—among them that of Lorenz, the Austrian ethologist (1952). For many years, he maintained a flock of jackdaws in his field laboratory. The birds were kept in absolute freedom most of the year, and Lorenz was able to learn a wealth of facts about their behavior. He observed that, unlike many other similar species, jackdaws do not recognize their enemies instinctively. They must learn who their enemies are from ". . . actual tradition, by the handing-down of personal experience from one generation to the next."

But jackdaws do react instinctively toward ". . . any living being that carries a black thing, dangling or fluttering"—a reaction possibly toward the generalized image of a jackdaw in the jaws or claws of a predator. When confronted with this sort of stimulus, the jackdaw makes a most raucous "rattling" cry of warning and attacks the apparent source of danger. Other jackdaws immediately join the onslaught on what has now been labeled "enemy." Lorenz reports being ". . . surrounded by a dense cloud of raging, rattling jackdaws, which hailed agonizing pecks upon my offending hand" just for pulling a pair of black bathing trunks out of his pocket.

After a rattling attack, the jackdaws who participated mistrust and hate the individual they attacked.

Provoke a jackdaw's rattling attack two or three times running and you have lost its friendship forever! From now on, it scolds as soon as it sees you, and you are branded, even when you are not carrying a black and fluttering object in your hands. And further, this jackdaw will easily succeed in convincing all the others of your guilt. Rattling is exceedingly infectious and stimulates its hearers to attack as promptly as does the sight of the black fluttering object in the clutches of the "enemy." The "evil gossip" that you have once or twice been seen carrying such an object, spreads like wildfire, and, almost before you know it, you are notorious amongst the jackdaws in the whole district as a beast of prey which must at all costs be combatted (p. 143).

[3] R. C. Jacobs and D. T. Campbell, The perpetuation of an arbitrary tradition through several generations of a laboratory microculture. *J. abnorm. soc. Psychol.*, 62, 649–658.

Lorenz observed that, by virtue of their social learning, young jack-daws acquire a blind and completely unreflecting behavior pattern. Even Lorenz himself, who was most sincerely interested in their welfare, could have been branded as their enemy. But he asked,

. . . have not we human beings also such blind, instinctive reactions? Do not whole peoples all too often react with a blind rage to a mere dummy presented to them by the artifice of the demagogue? Is not this dummy in many cases just as far from being a real enemy as were my black bathing drawers to the jackdaws? [4]

A typical example of "cultural" uniformities in animals are song "dialects" sometimes found among certain species of birds. Marler and Tamura (1964) were able to establish such a "dialect" among white-crowned sparrows in the laboratory. But what seems to be the most human-like instance was observed by Miyadi (1958). A group of Japanese monkeys, reared in a seminatural setting, was reported to have acquired the custom of washing sweet potatoes before eating them.

This processing method was first started in 1953 by a young female . . . It was first learned by her mother and play-fellow, and then by her sisters and brothers. At present [1958], many monkeys, especially the younger ones show the same behavior, which is expected to become a new cultural [sic] habit of this group in the future. There seems, however, little chance of propagation of new habits from one group to another, except possibly by solitary males, because Japanese monkey societies are well closed to members of other groups.

The above instances open the important possibility of experimental work on the introduction, transmission, and propagation of cultural uniformities—work which is almost entirely out of question with human cultures. While there are many difficulties with generalizing from animal to human behavior, the near future, no doubt, will see a rapid increase in the application of the experimental method to the study of culture.

SOCIAL DIFFERENTIATION

Take any collection of individuals who are strange and new to each other, let them interact, and if they survive as a group, you will observe the development of certain uniformities and differentiation. These uniformities deal with the relationships of the group members to the outside world—such as subsistence activities, cosmology, etc. Group differentiation applies primarily to the relationships of the individuals to one an-

[4] *King Solomon's Ring*, by Konrad Z. Lorenz. Copyright © 1952 by Thomas Y. Crowell Company, New York, Publishers. Reprinted with permission of author.

other. The experiment of Warren and Maroney (1958) discussed in Chapter 7 (pp. 78–81) is a good illustration of how social differentiation develops. Monkeys competing for food rapidly evolved a status hierarchy that showed a remarkable stability over a long time. Similar hierarchies are found among a host of other species, and they show similar stability.

Wynne-Edwards, in one of the most important recent contributions to animal ecology (1962), argued that dominance hierarchies in animal societies are the products of competition for food. The effect of a hierarchy is to maintain optimal population in a given habitat. Since the food resources of a given group of animals can be easily exhausted when the species overbreeds, the dominance hierarchy becomes an important feature of social organization, because it specifies food and breeding privileges for the individual members.

If there is a shortage of food, instead of this resulting in a general and uniform debilitation of all members of the society alike, and perhaps their ultimate extinction, the dominant animals are given a preferred chance of sustaining life and vigor throughout the period of famine, and thereafter multiplying and replenishing the stock. Their dominance behavior ensures that only as many as the remaining sources can sustain are allowed to partake of the food, and thus automatically the maximum number will survive; the excluded subordinates either perish quickly or emigrate to search for subsistence elsewhere. In a similar way, the successful individuals in reproduction are those that can hold their territorial status in the face of competition: those that cannot must again seek habitats elsewhere or refrain from breeding at all. *The function of the hierarchy, in fact, is always to identify the surplus individuals* whenever the population-density requires to be thinned out, and it has thus an extremely high survival value for the society as a whole (p. 139).[5]

Hierarchical structures exist whenever the demand for a certain commodity exceeds its supply, and whenever the social process has turned conflict over this commodity into competition regulated by conventional rules that define conventional privileges with respect to it. Food, territory, and breeding privileges—the most common objects of competition among animals—form the underlying bases of hierarchies among them. These "commodities" also constitute coveted though indirect goals of human competition; for instance, the demand for love and affection always exceeds supply.

The hierarchies that develop to "distribute" love and affection are as clearly structured and as stable as any others. In 1938 Moreno and Jennings examined such hierarchies in the New York State Training School

[5] Wynne-Edwards, 1962; reprinted with permission of author and publisher.

for Girls, using a procedure called *sociometry* first developed by Moreno in 1934 to describe various properties of groups. The girls in the Training School lived in cottages, each housing twenty-six inmates. The researchers studied seven of these cottages, asking the girls privately to indicate first, second, and third choices for their dining-table partners.

Table 10

Isolates, reciprocating pairs, and unreciprocated choices in seven cottages in the New York Training School for Girls. (From Sociometry, Vol. I, 1938, page 349, J. L. Moreno, M.O., Editor; Beacon House Inc., Publisher.)

COTTAGE NO.	ISOLATES	RECIPROCATING PAIRS	UNRECIPROCATING CHOICES
1	4	12	54
2	6	15	48
3	5	11	56
4	3	16	46
5	7	15	48
6	3	17	44
7	7	8	62
Average	5.0	13.4	51.1

Table 10 shows the number of isolates in each cottage (that is, girls not chosen at all), the number of reciprocating pairs, and the number of unreciprocated choices. One of the striking features of these sociometric findings is the structural similarity of the seven cottages. The number of isolates, for instance, is never less than three and never higher than seven, and the number of unreciprocated choices varies between forty-four and sixty-two.

We have proposed above that love is a commodity which invites rivalry and which is, as a consequence, distributed unequally among the members of a given group. We will therefore fail to see the full significance of these results if we do not ask what would be an "equal" distribution of love in these cottages; what should be expected by chance?

With each person having three choices, and with twenty-six girls in each cottage, the probability of one particular girl, i, being chosen by another particular girl, j, is three times out of twenty-five (because no girl chooses herself as a dining-table partner). (See Hays, 1966, for a discussion of probability theory.) The probability that i reciprocates and chooses j is equal to the product of two probabilities, $(3/25)^2$. If we wish to know what number of reciprocating pairs to expect by chance, we must simply multiply the probability of the given mutual choice by the number of pairs in the entire group, which is

$$\frac{26!}{2! \ (24)!} = 325.$$

Thus we would expect the average number of reciprocating pairs in a group of 26 girls to be $325(3/25)^2 = 4.68$. This figure is considerably lower than the one actually obtained. Even the cottage with the lowest number of mutuals had almost twice as many reciprocating pairs as we would expect by chance. This departure from a random structure is a *reciprocity bias*—a tendency of friends to choose each other.

It there is a greater-than-chance number of reciprocated choices, there must be in these groups also a smaller-than-chance number of un-reciprocated choices. The total number of all choices in a group of 26 is equal to $26 \times 3 = 78$. We have already determined that 4.68 of these will by chance be reciprocated. Thus, if we subtract 4.68 twice from 78 (because the figure refers to "pairs"), we will know the number of un-reciprocated choices to be expected by chance. We have $78 - 2(4.68) = 68.64$. As we suspected, the chance figure exceeds the obtained results.

Some girls are not chosen at all. What is the average number of these isolates one would expect by chance? Since the probability of the girl j being chosen by the girl i is $3/25$, the probability of j not being chosen by i is one minus that, or $22/25$. The probability that j is not chosen by i or by k is again $(22/25)^2$. The probability that j is not chosen by i, or by k, or by l is $(22/25)^3$, etc. Therefore, the probability that no one chooses j is exactly $(22/25)^{25}$, or .049. Since there are 26 girls altogether, we would expect an average of $26 \times .049 = 1.1$ isolates if the choices were made at random. We note from Table 6, however, that the number of isolates in the seven cottages is always higher. This excess of isolates in all seven groups over the number expected by chance lends support to our hypothesis that love, like other commodities, is distributed according to hierarchical arrangements.

When an observed set of sociograms systematically departs from one expected by chance, all in the same direction, we know that a "bias" governs the choices. This "bias" may be a greater-than-chance tendency to reciprocate a choice, as we have seen, or a tendency for the choices to favor especially a small subgroup of persons who choose each other or friends of friends, etc. The mathematical tools for analyzing biases in sociometric structures, dominance structures, and communication net-works are very useful in identifying underlying sociopsychological proc-esses (see Katz, 1952; Rapoport, 1963).

The reciprocity bias is apparently a rather pervasive and general feature of interpersonal relationships. So pervasive is this type of bias that an average person will tend implicitly to assume its existence for most "liking" relationships. Consider the following two hypothetical structures:

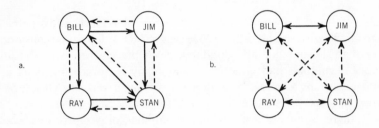

The solid arrow between Bill and Jim, pointing at Jim, means that Bill likes Jim. A broken arrow means that the source from which the arrow issues "dislikes" its destination. Thus in diagram (a) Jim dislikes Bill, while Jim and Ray dislike each other. We note that in (a) except for the reciprocal dislike between Ray and Jim, no relationships are reciprocated (double-headed arrows), while in (b) no relationships are unreciprocated. The following experiment by DeSoto (1960) illustrates the way people think about and perceive social relationships like these. Each of the lines of a given hypothetical structure, such as in (a) and (b), was printed on a card. On one side of the card was the name of the source and the destination of the arrow; the back of the card told whether the arrow was "positive" (that is, whether the source "liked" the destination) or "negative." The task of the subject was to learn what sort of an arrow was on the back of each of the twelve cards. He went through the set of cards several times, until he knew the exact connection between each of the six pairs of names. On every trial the subject was shown the front of the card and asked to say what was printed on the back. Whether or not he responded correctly, the back of the card was shown to him within a few seconds. The student may note that we are dealing here with the so-called paired-associates learning method (see Manis, 1966).

In one condition examined by DeSoto, an arrow meant "likes" and no arrow meant "dislikes." In this condition, the average subject required 14.7 trials to learn the complete structure (a)—which had no reciprocated relationships. However, the subjects required on the average only 10.9 trials to learn structure (b), whose relationships were all reciprocated. In another condition an arrow meant "influences" and no arrow meant "doesn't influence." In this condition, structures (a) and (b) required 8.9 and 12.9 trials respectively. A given hypothetical structure can be learned more easily if it represents the sort of biases that characterize actual social structures. Our social experience, apparently, leads us to think that "liking" relationships always have a reciprocity bias. When the only information we have indicates that Bill likes Jim, we are more likely to assume that Jim also likes Bill than that he dislikes him (DeSoto and Kuethe, 1959). Influence and dominance structures, on the other hand, are generally thought of as having an antireciprocity bias. If Bill has some influence over Jim, then we believe it unlikely that Jim has also influence over Bill. These "social schemata" account for the differences in the learning of the hypothetical social structures constructed by DeSoto.

Heider (1946) identified and analyzed another sort of bias that characterizes the perceptions we have of social relationships. In a three-person group—Bill, Jim, and Ray—if Bill likes Jim and Ray, then he will be pleased to know that Jim also likes Ray. Heider described such states as *balanced*. But if Bill learns that Jim dislikes Ray, he might be a bit disturbed. The more Jim and Ray are important to him, the more he will worry about the relationship between them. Such states are *unbalanced*. People avoid unbalanced states or attempt to restore balance.

Cartwright and Harary (1956) defined balanced states more precisely. For example when all relationships in a three-person group are mutual, balance occurs if the number of mutual dislikes is even; otherwise the group is unbalanced. In the four diagrams below, where the solid and broken arrows mean as before "likes" and "dislikes" respectively, groups (a) and (b) are balanced, while groups (c) and (d) are unbalanced.[6]

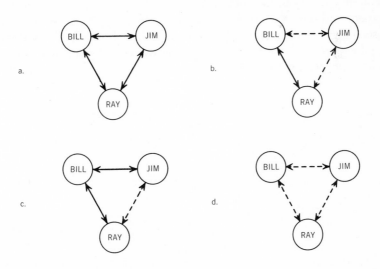

[6] For large groups complex procedures must be used to determine balance. These procedures are discussed in Cartwright and Harary (1956).

While Heider's theory relates primarily to the way people perceive and think about social relationships, Newcomb (1953) found empirical support for this theory in actual social groupings. However, Jordan (1953), Morrissette (1958), and others have shown that people's perceptions of interpersonal relationships are indeed characterized by a balance bias. More recently Zajonc and Burnstein (1965) studied this perceptual bias using the learning technique developed by DeSoto. They found that subjects made consistently fewer errors in learning balanced structures than in learning unbalanced ones. They also found, however, that positive relationships ("likes," "approves of," etc.) are easier to learn than negative ones ("dislikes," "disapproves of"). Thus, a "positivity" bias apparently also exists in the perception of interpersonal relationships.

This chapter considered two kinds of consequences of social interaction: uniformity and differentiation. Two points must have become apparent in our discussion, although we have not stressed them explicitly. First, while uniformities and differentiation do indeed result from interaction, they are at the same time the very basis upon which social interaction can take place. No prolonged social relationship can be maintained without some uniformity. Even the relationship between a dog and his master requires it: the dog shares the "meaning" of the master's calls and orders, and even deadly enemies understand each other's threats.

The other point to be made is that uniformity and differentiation are considerably more complex concepts than either social behavior or social interaction and must be studied with analytical techniques of greater refinement and power. Here we must appeal for help to related fields, such as sociology, anthropology, economics, political science, ecology, and ethnology—all of which provide various ways of dealing with the morphology of social structures.

ARE TWO HEADS BETTER THAN ONE?

Uniformity and differentiation are rather abstract consequences of social interaction. The group process, however, also generates a concrete consequence: the group product. Innumerable concrete achievements are credited not to particular individuals but to groups, teams, assemblies, committees, commissions, councils, communities, companies, corporations, trusts, unions, governments, parliaments, parties, courts, juries, churches, armies, gangs, and the like. The achievements claimed by a group are often assumed to surpass the sum of achievements of an equal number of isolated individuals and, certainly, those of a single individual. Two heads are better than one, we say. But are they?

In 1924 Gordon had 200 subjects, working alone, rank ten weights. The weights differed from each other by small amounts, so that judgment was difficult. Each subject's ordering was then correlated with the true order. These rank correlations were then averaged over the 200 subjects, resulting in a mean correlation of .41. This correlation was taken as an index of individual accuracy of judgments. In order to determine whether many heads are better than one, the following procedure was undertaken. The 200 rankings were randomly grouped into sets of five. Each set of five rankings was averaged, thus generating forty rank orders. Each of these forty orders was correlated with the true order as before. The average of these forty correlation coefficients was .68—an index of accuracy of judgments for the combined judgment of five persons. In a like manner hypothetical "groups" of ten, twenty, and fifty were created; indexes of accuracy were obtained for all such groups.[1]

For "groups" of ten subjects the average rank correlation was .79, for groups of twenty .86, and for groups of fifty subjects (there were, of course, only four such groups) the average rank correlation was .94. Gordon concluded that ". . . the results of the group are distinctly superior to the results of the average member and are equal to those of the best members." Table 11 summarizes the findings of Gordon and of five other researchers who obtained similar results.

But before we agree that group judgments are superior to individual

[1] The student should keep in mind that all judgments were made by single individuals working alone. When Gordon spoke of "groups," she meant sets of judgments selected at random by the experimenter.

Table 11

The reliability of judgments of individuals and of groups.

TYPE OF JUDGMENT AND AUTHOR	INDI-VIDUALS	SIZE OF GROUP					
		5	10	20	40	50	60
Weights: Gordon, 1924	.41	.68	.79	.86		.94	
Weights: Stroop, 1932	.38	.68	.85	.92		.96	
Weights: Bruce, 1935	.50	.67	.83	.86	.87		.88
Numerosity of shot: Bruce, 1935	.82	.87	.94	.94	.94		.95
Personality traits: Smith, 1931	.37	.46	.49	.49		.51	
Esthetic judgments: Eysenck, 1939	.47	.77	.86	.94		.98	

ones, let us perform an imaginary experiment. Suppose we have five areas, A, B, C, D, E—all threatened with flood. We send observers to evaluate the relative threat in these areas, so that help may be deployed most efficiently. One of the observers, W, comes back with the report that the order of threat is A, C, B, E, D; the second, X, and the third observer, Y, both judge it D, E, B, C, A; and the last, Z, ranks the five areas E, C, D, A, B. Since the observers do not agree, and since we "know" from Table 11 that the group judgments are more reliable than individual ones, we average individual rankings.

Table 12 shows the average individual rankings of threat. Suppose that in actuality, the greatest threat exists for area A, second greatest for B, then for C, then D, and finally the threat in area E is negligible. But if we follow the group judgment, we shall deploy our heaviest resources to the area that needs help the least, while the area needing help immediately will be the last on our schedule. As a matter of fact, our schedule for flood prevention is almost a perfectly inverse function of urgency, the average rank correlation between the true order and the averaged rankings being —.100. Yet no individual observer's judgment was so far from reality. Instead of averaging the ranks, if we had simply selected one of the four orders at random, the worst we could have done is —.80. In fact, we would have had one chance in four of coming up with a fairly accurate estimate of danger (observer W's).

This is not just an exception to Gordon's conclusion. Her conclusion was wrong. Combined individual judgments will surpass individual

Table 12

Individual and group judgments:
a hypothetical example.

THREAT AREAS	TRUE ORDER	INDIVIDUAL OBSERVER'S RANKS				SUM OF RANKS	AVERAGE RANK
		W	X	Y	Z		
A	1	1	5	5	4	15	5
B	2	3	3	3	5	14	4
C	3	2	4	4	2	12	3
D	4	5	1	1	3	10	2
E	5	4	2	2	1	9	1

Individual rank correlation .80 −.80 −.80 −.80
Average rank correlation ($\bar{r}_{kg}$) −.40
Correlation with the average rank (r_{kg}^{-}) −1.00

judgments *only* if a majority of the individuals making judgments have a fair chance of being correct. To put it differently, if most of the correlations between individual orders and the true order are positive, then Gordon's conclusion holds. If, however, the correlations are negative, as in Table 12, then the combined judgments will be worse than those of single individuals. Stroop (1932) was first to notice a possibility of an error in Gordon's work, but the complete explication of the problem was not achieved until later (Eysenck, 1939; Zajonc, 1962).

The above results can be predicted from a general formula.[2] Briefly, the correlation of an average order with the true order, $r_{\bar{k}g}$, can be indicated as follows:

$$r_{\bar{k}g} = \frac{n\bar{r}_{kg}}{\sqrt{n + n(n-1)\bar{r}_{kk'}}}.$$

r_{kg} is the average correlation between individual orders and the true order (for the example in Table 12 it was −.40); $\bar{r}_{kk'}$ is the average intercorrelation between individual orders; and n is the size of the group.[3] If individual judges are primarily wrong—that is, if $\bar{r}_{kg}$ is negative in the equation—the correlation between the average of their individual judgments and the true order, $r_{\bar{k}g}$, will also be negative. In general, in this case we will expect $r_{\bar{k}g}$ to be closer than $\bar{r}_{kg}$ to −1.00 (a perfectly inverse relationship).

The immediate significance of our discussion is to illustrate the relative power of generalizations based on a hasty observation and on

[2] Students not familiar with correlational techniques may wish to skip this and the next paragraph.
[3] The bars over the symbols indicate whether judgments ($\bar{k}$) or correlations ($\bar{r}$) are being averaged. The student should note that the formula applies to the Pearson-Product-Moment Correlation rather than to the rank correlations used in the present example.

theory. Gordon's conclusion that groups are superior to individuals is based on one set of observations. But what follows from the theoretical formula? It might be instructive to attempt to predict the variety of results shown in Table 11. The only unknown quantity is $r_{kk'}$, the average intercorrelation among the individual judges. Estimates of $r_{kk'}$ (calculated by the least squares method) are for Gordon's results .180, for Stroop's .128, for Bruce's .300 (weights) and .772 (shot), for Smith's .510, and for Eysenck's .210. Students who wish may fairly accurately predict each of the obtained results in Table 11, which seem to illustrate group superiority. The formula, however, also predicts the result in Table 12, which leads to the opposite conclusion.

Two judgments are then better than one if each is better than chance. If each is worse than chance, then one is better than two. We will qualify this generalization after we have examined other comparisons of individual and group productivity. This type of comparison dates from the early days of social psychology, although it then involved a somewhat different emphasis. Triplett's question, for instance, was not whether a group is superior to an individual, or to a collection of isolated individuals, but whether the individual's own performance changes when he works in a group. The first three chapters dealt with this problem, and the answer to it was not a simple "yes" or "no."

The research on individual and group judgments which we have just examined also lead us to believe that the answers to "division-of-labor" problems are not simple either. Ringelmann, a German industrial psychologist, found that a single person could pull on the average an equivalent of 63 kg (Dashiell, 1935, pp. 1113–1114). Two persons together could pull an equivalent of 118 kg, three 160 kg, and eight 248 kg. Two pairs of hands here were better than one pair but only in a very limited sense. One person all by himself could lift 63 kg, *but two people accomplished less than twice as much*, and three people less than three times as much, and eight people considerably less than eight times as much. If each individual had been contributing his full potential (that is, 63 kg) in the group situation, then an eight-person group should have been able to pull an equivalent of 504 kg. In actuality, the eight-person group pulled, according to Ringelmann, not quite half of this quantity.

If we assume than in the "alone" situation the individual worked at 100 percent (certainly an overestimation), then in a two-person group he contributed only 93 percent of what he could do all by himself. In a three-person group each individual seemed to be working at 85 percent of his "alone" capacity, and in the eight-person group each member worked at only 49 percent. With every additional person added to the group, the members reduced their contribution by about 7 percent of their potential. Extrapolating, we obtain the preposterous result that members would work at nearly zero capacity in a fourteen-person group. The simplified equation for predicting the percentage of individual capacity contributed (c) as a function of group size (n) is $c = 100\% - 7n$. Thus, for $c = 0$, we must have $n = 14.3$. If we consider the increased actual weight pulled, adding new persons in fact results in a greater group product. But we gain increasingly less with each new person added. If we were to pay, let us say, $10.00 for each person's labor, then we would be paying twice as much per kg lifted in an eight-person group (that is, 32¢) than for an individual by himself (16¢). It appears that the loss in individual contributions is due to increasing difficulty in coordinating the individual efforts into a joint product as the group increases. To cumulate efforts optimally, the individuals would have to pull at exactly the same time, in exactly the same direction, and without otherwise interfering with one another.

To make meaningful comparisons between group and individual performance, the way in which individual contributions are combined into a joint product must be known precisely. For example let us say that the Security Council of the United Nations must decide whether troops should be sent to a war-threatened country. Let us further assume that there is in fact a best decision, and that each member of the Council has a certain probability of reaching it. Let us assume that this probability, p, is equal for all Council members and that it is fixed at .90. Since the Security Council operates by means of unanimity, all members must vote "correctly" for the Council as a body to be correct. If we assume that the votes of the Council members are independent of one another (as fictional as the value p), then the probability that the Council will reach the "correct" decision is the product of the individual probabilities, or $p^{11} = .90^{11} = .31$, since the Security Council seats eleven members. Thus, while each individual member is able to reach the correct decision nine out of ten times, the Council's record is not better than one out of three. If the Security Council had 100 instead of eleven members, and if each member would vote "correctly" 90 percent of the time, then we would have a "correct" decision from the Security Council once in about 40,000 times! [4]

[4] What would be the likelihood of the Security Council's reaching a correct decision if it operated under, let us say, a majority rule, instead of the unanimity rule? Under the conditions of our hypothetical example (that is, individual members have nine out of ten chances of voting "correctly"), the Council would then seldom reach an incorrect decision. For a discussion of this conclusion and the mathematics of group decision making, see Smoke and Zajonc (1962) where various group decision schemes are analyzed according to the reliability they promise. Suffice it to say now that the formula for the probability that a group under majority rule will be correct is

$$\sum_{i=m}^{n} \binom{i}{n} p^i (1-p)^{n-i},$$

where p is the probability of an individual member being correct, n the size of the group, and m the majority in question (such as ½ n or ¾ n).

In actual groups, responsibility is seldom the same for all group members, their ability is almost never equal, and the task assignments they receive are seldom of equal importance, equal difficulty, and often quite difficult to compare with one another. Still, the scheme for combining individual outputs into a group product sets limits within which group performance can vary. The major factors that influence group performance within these limits are division of labor and the distribution of ability among the members.

OPTIMAL DIVISION OF LABOR

Given a particular task and group, an optimal division of labor exists. If the United States Post Office had all employees sorting mail, and the Postmaster General alone delivering it, there would be many dissatisfied taxpayers. No doubt the division of labor the United States Post Office now maintains is superior to the one hypothetically suggested. But are we sure that it is the best possible? How can we objectively evaluate various types of division of labor and find the most efficient for a group task? Our previous experience with Gordon's results in examining the relative merits of group and individual performance teaches us that the empirical approach alone may not be the most fruitful one here. Let us then look at a theoretical approach to the problem (Zajonc and Smoke, 1959). Imagine that we have three spies, X, Y, and Z, who have come upon three very important and rather involved items of intelligence, A, B, and C. Since they cannot write the information down, and momentarily have no means of relaying it to their superiors, they must simply memorize it. They want each item to be remembered by at least one of them. They do not care who remembers what, as long as all the intelligence they gathered can be recovered at the proper time. How shall X, Y, and Z assign the three items A, B, and C among themselves so that the likelihood of each item being recovered intact is highest? We may give all three items to all spies. We may give one item to each. Or we may give A and B to X, B and C to Y, and A and C to Z. We may even have a more complex division of labor, such as assigning A, B, and C to X, A and B to Y, and C to Z, or any variants of these. Is there a division of labor superior to all others, and, if so, what is it?

Consider the problem in somewhat more general terms. Assume that we have a group of N individuals and H items of information. We wish each item to have the highest probability of being recovered from the group as a whole; and we consider that the item is remembered "by the group" if at least one individual remembers it. How should these H items be assigned to our N people?

Intuition and research tell us that the more items we assign to a given person, the less likely it is that he will remember any given one. For instance, if one must learn and remember 100 telephone numbers, the probability that he remembers a particular number after some time is relatively small. The probability that he remembers it is considerably greater when he is assigned only one or two telephone numbers in addition to it. On the basis of this consideration, it would be best to assign as few of the H items as possible to each of the N people. But if we wish each item to have the highest probability of being recalled by at least one group member, we may be tempted to assign each item to as large a number of persons as possible. But then each person will have to remember a very large number of items—a condition that we just agreed to avoid.

To solve our problem we must impose some restrictions. First let us agree that the probability that a given individual will remember a given item is equal to p, which is the same for all group members and for all items of information. Second, each individual member receives h items to retain—the same for all members. And, finally, each item will be assigned to an equal number of individuals, n.

Now the probability that an individual will forget a given item he was asked to remember is just $1 - p$. Consequently, the probability that all n individuals to whom that item was assigned will forget it is $(1 - p)^n$, since we also assume that the group members do not influence each other's recall. However, we are interested in the probability that the given item be remembered by at least one of those to whom it was assigned. That probability, P, is equal to $1 - (1 - p)^n$.

Our original question about what is the optimal assignment of items now becomes the question of what should n equal to so that P may be at its highest.[5] Students who have had calculus will realize that we are dealing here with a problem of a maximum—specifically the maximum value of P as a function of n. We must, therefore, find the derivative of P with respect to n, set it equal to zero, and solve for n.

The derivative of P with respect to n is not simply of the form $du^n = nu^{n-1} du$, because n and p are related. We do know that p is some function of h, and under the present restrictions

$$h = n \frac{H}{N}.$$

Hence, n cannot be treated as an independent exponent. The derivative dP/dn is rather of the form $du^v = vu^{v-1}du + u^v \log_e u\, dv$, where u and v are interrelated. We have thus

$$\frac{dP}{dn} = \frac{d\,[1 - (1 - p)^n]}{dn} = 0,$$

$$= -\frac{d(1 - p)^n}{dn} = 0,$$

$$= -n(1 - p)^{n-1}\left[\frac{d(1 - p)}{dn}\right] + (1 - p)^n \log_e(1 - p) = 0,$$

$$= n(1 - p)^{n-1}\left(\frac{dp}{dn}\right) - (1 - p)^n \log_e(1 - p) = 0,$$

Factoring $(1 - p)^n$ we obtain

$$\frac{dP}{dn} = (1 - p)^n\left[\frac{dp}{dn}\left(\frac{n}{1 - p}\right) - \log_e(1 - p)\right] = 0.$$

Now, unless p is equal to unity, the above derivative can be equal to zero only if the bracketed expression is equal to zero. Thus, we need to consider only

$$(1) \qquad \frac{dp}{dn}\left(\frac{n}{1 - p}\right) - \log_e(1 - p) = 0.$$

We can now find the value of n, which will give us a maximum P, provided we know the relationship between p and n. Only a suggestion was made thus far that the probability of an item being remembered by a given member, p, decreases with the number of items assigned to him. Knowing that n is a function of h, let us find, preferably from some unknown empirical data, a function which relates p to h and which, incidentally, will allow us to find dp/dn without too much difficulty. A reasonable function is

$$p = e^{-k^2 h^2},$$

where k is an empirical constant reflecting perhaps the difficulty of the items. This function fits, for instance, data on recall collected by Oberly (1928) with $k = .10$. If that is the function relating p to h, then

$$(2) \qquad \frac{dp}{dn} = \frac{d(e^{-k^2 h^2})}{dn} = e^{-k^2 h^2}(-k^2)\frac{dh^2}{dn} = e^{-k^2 h^2}(-k^2)\,2h\,\frac{dh}{dn}.$$

But under the conditions we required of the problem, $h = n(H/N)$. Hence,

$$\frac{dh}{dn} = \frac{dn}{dn}\left(\frac{H}{N}\right) + \left(\frac{dH/N}{dn}\right)n,$$

and since H/N is constant,

$$\frac{dh}{dn} = \frac{H}{N}.$$

Sustituting in (2) we have,

(3) $$\frac{dp}{dn} = e^{-k^2h^2} (-k^2) 2h(H/N).$$

Finally, substituting (3) in equation (1), we have

$$\frac{n[-e^{-k^2h^2}(k^2)2h(H/N)]}{1-p} - \log_e(1-p) = 0,$$

and since $n(H/N) = h$, and $e^{-k^2h^2} = p$ and therefore $-k^2h^2 = \log_e p$, we obtain

(4) $$\frac{2p \log_e p}{1-p} - \log_e(1-p) = 0,$$

which solves for $p = .84$.

(*) The solution (4) we obtained tells us that the maximum value of P will be obtained if p, the probability that a given individual recalls a given item among those he was assigned, is equal to .84. In other words, we will have the most efficient division of labor if each individual is assigned a number of items which will result in his remembering only 84 percent of them. Now, since we know the relation between p and h, and since n is a function of h, we can also find the optimal values of h and n. First, how many items should we assign to each person? Since we decided that

$$p = e^{-k^2h^2} \text{ and } h = \sqrt{\log_e p/-k^2},$$

and since $p = .84$, the optimal value of h is $.42/k$, where k is an empirical constant depending on the difficulty of the items. The highest likelihood of a given item being remembered by at least one person results when each person is assigned $.42/k$ items. With the constant k equal to .10, as was the case in the data from which the function relating p to h was derived (Oberly, 1928), the optimal assignment is 4.2 items per person. Note that the results with respect to optimal values of p and h are *independent* of the size of the group, N, and of the magnitude of the group task, H. The solution tells us namely that we should overload our group members by 16 percent, regardless of how many of them make up the group, and regardless of how much total work there is—a curious result that we would not suspect intuitively. Of course, the number of people to which each item is assigned (n) will vary with the size of the group and the size of the group task. The larger the group, the more people who can be assigned the given item. We have from previous conditions $n = h(N/H)$ and hence optimum n is

$$\frac{.42/k}{N/H}.$$

Thus, for instance, if the constant k is equal to .10, as in the data of Oberly (1928), and if we have the same number of people as there are items to remember, then each item should be assigned to four persons. This amount of redundancy in task assignment will produce the most efficient recall pattern. It may incidentally be noted that our result with respect to the optimal value of p is also independent of individual differences in recall. Zajonc and Smoke (1959) have shown that when group members differ in ability to remember items, and if each individual is overloaded by 16 percent, each item will have the highest probability of being recalled. Under these conditions, however, the number of items assigned to each individual will vary according to his ability to remember them. Group members known to have relatively good recall will receive more items, while those who can remember less will receive fewer items. Still, the solution obtained recommends assigning to each individual a number of items which would exceed his recall ability by 16 percent.

Our analysis illustrates the usefulness of a mathematical application to social-psychological problems. It would take considerably more effort to solve the problem of optimal task assignments by means of empirical methods—that is, by varying one variable after another and observing the effects. However, the mathematical solution provides only a *general* answer—that is, the solution is true in the absolute sense, subject only to the restrictions specified in the formulation of the problem. Although these conditions may not be met in life, the mathematical solution can serve as a standard against which empirical results can be compared. If our empirical observations conflict with it, the mathematical solution shows us where to look in order to explain *why* the empirical results do not conform to theoretical expectations.

We tried to accomplish in this chapter two rather independent purposes. First, while tracing various ways in which the group product may depend on the individual outputs of group members, we attempted to show how research problems about group productivity are formulated. Second, we took examples from the work on group productivity to underscore the value of mathematics in social psychology. The mathematical approach is a recent development (Criswell, Solomon, and Suppes, 1962; Luce, Bush, and Galanter, 1963), but it has already shown considerable promise. It is almost certain that mathematics will be used increasingly in social psychology.

REFERENCES

Adams, J. S., and Hoffman, D. The frequency of self-reference statements as a function of generalized reinforcement. *J. abnorm. soc. Psychol.*, 1960, *60*, 384–389.

Ader, R., and Tatum, R. Free-operant avoidance conditioning in individual and paired human subjects. *J. exp. anal. Beh.*, 1963, *6*, 357–359.

Adorno, T. W., Frenkel-Brunswik, E., Levinson, D. J., and Sanford, R. N. *The authoritarian personality.* New York: Harper, 1950.

Allee, W. C., and Masure, R. H. A comparison of maze behavior in paired and isolated shell parakeets (*Melopsittacus Undulatus*, Shaw). *Physiol. Zool.*, 1936, *22*, 131–56.

Allport, F. H. The influence of the group upon association and thought. *J. exper. Psychol.*, 1920, *3*, 159–182.

————. *Social psychology.* Boston: Houghton Mifflin, 1924.

Allyn, J., and Festinger, L. The effectiveness of unanticipated persuasive communications. *J. abnorm. soc. Psychol.*, 1961, *62*, 35–40.

Asch, S. *Social psychology.* New York: Prentice-Hall, 1952.

Bandura, A., and McDonald, F. J. Influence of social reinforcement and the behavior of models in shaping children's moral judgments. *J. abnorm. soc. Psychol.*, 1963, *67*, 274–281.

Berger, S. M. Conditioning through vicarious instigation. *Psychol. Rev.*, 1962, *69*, 450–466.

Bergum, B. O., and Lehr, D. J. Effects of authoritarianism on vigilance performance. *J. appl. Psychol.*, 1963, *47*, 75–77.

Birch, J. D., and Veroff, J. *Motivation: A study of action.* Belmont, Calif.: Wadsworth, 1966.

Bixenstine, V. E., Potash, H. M., and Wilson, K. V. Effects of level of co-operative choice by the other player on choices in a Prisoner's Dilemma game. Part I. *J. abnorm. soc. Psychol.*, 1963, *66*, 308–313.

Bixenstine, V. E., and Wilson, K. V. Effects of level of cooperative choice by the other player on choices in a Prisoner's Dilemma game. Part II. *J. abnorm. soc. Psychol.*, 1963, *67*, 139–147.

Blake, R. R., Helson, H., and Mouton, J. S. The generality of conformity behavior as a function of factual anchorage, difficulty of task, and amount of social pressure. *J. Pers.*, 1956, *25*, 294–305.

Bruce, R. H. An experimental analysis of social factors affecting the performance of white rats. I. Performance in learning in a simple field situation. *J. comp. Psychol.*, 1941, *31*, 363–377.

Bruce, R. S. Group judgments in the fields of lifted weights and visual discrimination. *J. Psychol.*, 1935, *1*, 117–121.

Cantril, H. *Gauging public opinion.* Princeton, N.J.: Princeton Univ. Press, 1944.

Cartwright, D., and Harary, F. Structural balance: A generalization of Heider's theory. *Psychol. Rev.*, 1956, *63*, 277–293.

Centers, R. A laboratory adaptation of the controversial procedure for the conditioning of verbal operants. *J. abnorm. soc. Psychol.*, 1963, *67*, 334–339.

Chen, S. C. Social modification of the activity of ants in nest-building. *Physiol. Zool.*, 1937, *10*, 420–436.

Church, R. M. Transmission of learned behavior between rats. *J. abnorm. soc. Psychol.*, 1957, *54*, 163–165.

Criswell, J., Solomon, H., and Suppes, P. (Eds.). *Mathematical methods in small group processes.* Stanford, Calif.: Stanford Univ. Press, 1962.

Crutchfield, R. S. The measurement of individual conformity to group opinion among officer personnel. Institute of Personality Assessment and Research. Univ. of California, Berkeley, *Res. Bull.*, 1954.

————. Conformity and character. *Amer. Psychologist*, 1955, *10*, 191–198.

Darby, C. L., and Riopelle, A. J. Observational learning in rhesus monkey. *J. comp. physiol. Psychol.*, 1959, *52*, 94–98.

Darwin, C. *The descent of man.* New York: Appleton, 1871.

Dashiell, J. F. An experimental analysis of some group effects. *J. abnorm. soc. Psychol.*, 1930, *25*, 190–199.

————. Experimental studies of the influence of social situations on the behavior of individual human adults. In Murchison, C. (Ed.), *A handbook of social psychology.* Worcester, Mass.: Clark Univ. Press, 1935.

DeSoto, C. B. Learning a social structure. *J. abnorm. soc. Psychol.*, 1960, *60*, 417–421.

DeSoto, C. B., and Kuethe, J. L. Subjective probabilities of interpersonal relationships. *J. abnorm. soc. Psychol.*, 1959, *59*, 290–294.

Deutsch, M., and Gerard, H. B. A study of normative and informational social influences upon individual judgment. *J. abnorm. soc. Psychol.*, 1955, *51*, 629–636.

Dobzhansky, T. *Evolution, genetics, and man.* New York: Wiley, 1955.

Espinas, A. *Des sociétés animales.* Paris: Bailliere, 1878.

Etkin, W. (Ed.). *Social behavior and organization among vertebrates.* Chicago: Univ. of Chicago Press, 1964.

Eysenck, H. J.   The validity of judgments as a function of the number of judges. *J. exp. Psychol.*, 1939, *25*, 650–654.

Festinger, L.   Informal social communication. *Psychol. Rev.*, 1950, *57*, 271–292.

Festinger, L., Back K., Schachter, S. Kelley, H. H., and Thibaut, J.   *Theory and experiment in social communication.* Ann Arbor, Mich.: Research Center for Group Dynamics, 1950.

Festinger, L., and Maccoby, N.   On resistance to persuasive communications. *J. abnorm. soc. Psychol.*, 1964, *68*, 359–366.

Festinger, L., and Thibaut, J.   Interpersonal communication in small groups. *J. abnorm. soc. Psychol.*, 1951, *46*, 92–99.

Fitts, P. M., and Posner, M.   *Human performance.* Belmont, Calif.: Wadsworth (in press).

von Frisch, Karl.   *Bees: Their vision, chemical senses, and language.* Ithaca, N.Y.: Cornell Univ. Press, 1950.

Gates, M. G., and Allee, W. C.   Conditioned behavior of isolated and grouped cockroaches on a simple maze. *J. comp. Psychol.*, 1933, *13*, 331–358.

Gordon, K. H.   Group judgments in the field of lifted weights. *J. exp. Psychol.*, 1924, *3*, 398–400.

Greenspoon, T.   The reinforcing effect of two spoken sounds on the frequency of two responses. *Amer. J. Psychol.*, 1955, *68*, 409–416.

Gurnee, H.   The effect of collective learning upon the individual participants. *J. abnorm. soc. Psychol.*, 1939, *34*, 529–532.

Guthrie, E. R.   *The psychology of learning.* New York: Harper, 1952.

Haney, W. V.   Serial communication of information in organizations. *ETC.*, 1964, *21*, 13–29.

Harlow, H. F.   Social facilitation of feeding in the albino rat. *J. genet. Psychol.*, 1932, *43*, 211–221.

Hays, W. L.   *Quantification in psychology.* Belmont, Calif.: Wadsworth, 1966.

Heider, F.   Attitudes and cognitive organization. *J. Psychol.*, 1946, *21*, 107–112.

Helvetius, C. A.   *A treatise on man.* London: Albion Press, 1810.

Herbert, M. J., and Harsh, C. H.   Observational learning in cats. *J. comp. Psychol.*, 1944, *37*, 81–95.

Hess, E.   Imprinting and the "critical period" concept. In Bliss, E. L. (Ed.), *Roots of behavior.* New York: Harper, 1962.

Hildum, D. C., and Brown, R. W.   Verbal reinforcement and interviewer bias. *J. abnorm. soc. Psychol.*, 1956, *53*, 108–111.

Horwitz, M.   The recall of interrupted group tasks: An experimental study of individual motivation in relation to group goals. *Hum. Relat.*, 1954, *7*, 3–38.

Hovland, C. I., Janis, I. L., and Kelley, H. H. *Communication and persuasion.* New Haven, Conn.: Yale Univ. Press, 1953.

Husband, R. W. Analysis of methods in human maze learning. *J. genet. Psychol.*, 1931, *39*, 258–277.

Iscoe, I., Williams, M. S., and Harvey, J. Modification of children's judgments by a simulated group technique: A normative, developmental study. *Child Develpm.* 1963, *34*, 963–978.

Jacobs, R. C., and Campbell, D. T. The perpetuation of an arbitrary tradition through several generations of a laboratory microculture. *J. abnorm. soc. Psychol.*, 1961, *62*, 649–658.

James, W. T. The development of social facilitation of eating in puppies. *J. genet. Psychol.*, 1960, *96*, 123–127.

Jones, E. E., Wells, H. H., and Torrey, R. Some effects of feedback from the experimenter on conformity behavior. *J. abnorm. soc. Psychol.*, 1958, *57*, 207–213.

Jordan, N. Behavioral forces that are a function of attitudes and of cognitive organization. *Hum. Relat.*, 1953, *6*, 273–287.

Katz, Daniel. Do interviewers bias poll results? *Publ. Opin. Quart.*, 1942, *6*, 248–268.

Katz, David. *Animals and men.* London: Longmans, Green and Co., 1937.

Katz, L. The distribution of the number of isolates in a social group. *Ann. math. Statist.*, 1952, *23*, 271–276.

Kelley, H. H., Thibaut, J. W., Radloff, R., and Mundy, D. The development of cooperation in the "minimal social situation." *Psychol. Mon.*, 1962, *76* (19, Whole No. 538).

Klopfer, P. H. Influence of social interaction on learning rates in birds. *Science*, 1958, *128*, 903.

Le Bon, G. *The crowd: A study of the popular mind.* London: T. Fisher Unwin, 1896.

Lewis, H. B. An experimental study of the role of the ego in work. I. The role of the ego in cooperative work. *J. exp. Psychol.*, 1944, *34*, 113–126.

Lorenz, K. *King Solomon's ring.* New York: Crowell, 1952.

Luce, R. D., Bush, R. B., and Galanter, E. (Eds.). *Handbook of mathematical psychology.* New York: Wiley, 1963.

Manis, M. *Cognitive processes.* Belmont, Calif.: Wadsworth, 1966.

Marler, P., and Tamura, M. Culturally transmitted patterns of vocal behavior in sparrows. *Science*, 1964, *146*, 1483–1486.

Mason, J. W., and Brady, J. V. The sensitivity of psychoendocrine systems to social and physical environment. In Leiderman, P., and Shapiro, D. (Eds.), *Psychobiological approaches to social behavior.* Stanford, Calif.: Stanford Univ. Press, 1964.

Meumann, E. Haus- und Schularbeit: Experimente an Kindern der Volksschule. *Die Deutsche Schule*, 1904, *8*, 278–303, 337–359, 416–431.

Milgram, S. Nationality and conformity. *Sci. Amer.*, 1961, *205*, 45–51.

Miller, N. E., and Dollard, J. *Social learning and imitation.* New Haven, Conn.: Yale Univ. Press, 1941.

Miller, R. E., Banks, J. H., Jr., and Ogawa, N. Communication of affect in "cooperative conditioning" of rhesus monkeys. *J. abnorm. soc. Psychol.*, 1962, *64*, 343–348.

——————. Role of facial expression in "cooperative-avoidance conditioning" in monkeys. *J. abnorm. soc Psychol.*, 1963, 67, 24–30.

Minas, J. S., Scodel, A., Marlowe, D., and Rawson, H. Some descriptive aspects of two-person, non-zero sum games. Part II. *J. conflict Resolut.*, 1960, *4*, 193–197.

Miyadi, D. On some new habits and their propagation in Japanese monkey groups. *Proceedings XV Int. Cong. Zool.*, London, 1958, 857–861.

Moreno, J. L. *Who shall survive?* Boston: Beacon House, 1934.

Moreno, J. L., and Jennings, H. H. Statistics of social configurations. *Sociometry*, 1938, *1*, 342–374.

Morrissette, J. An experimental study of the theory of structural balance. *Hum. Relat.*, 1958, *11*, 239–254.

Murphy, J. V., Miller, R. E., and Mirsky, I. A., Inter-animal conditioning in the monkey. *J. comp. physiol. Psychol.*, 1955, *48*, 211–214.

Newcomb, T. M. An approach to the study of communicative acts. *Psychol. Rev.*, 1953, *60*, 393–404.

Nuthmann, A. M. Conditioning of a response class on a personality test. *J. abnorm. soc. Psychol.*, 1957, *54*, 19–23.

Oberly, H. S. A comparison of the spans of "attention" and memory. *Amer. J. Psychol.*, 1928, *40*, 295–302.

Pessin, J. The comparative effects of social and mechanical stimulation on memorizing. *Amer. J. Psychol.*, 1933, *45*, 263–270.

Piaget, J. *The moral judgment of the child.* Glencoe, Ill.: Free Press, 1948.

Rapoport, A. Mathematical theory of motivation interactions between two individuals: I. *Bull. Math. Biophysics*, 1947, *9*, 17–28. (a)

——————. Mathematical theory of motivation interactions between two individuals: I. *Bull. Math. Biophysics*, 1947, *9*, 41–61. (b)

——————. Mathematical models of social interaction. In Luce, R. D., Bush, R. B., and Galanter, E. (Eds.), *Handbook of mathematical psychology.* New York: Wiley, 1963.

Rasmussen, E. W. Social facilitation in albino rats. *Acta Psychol.*, 1939, *4*, 275–294.

Rousseau, J. J. *Émile.* New York: Appleton & Co., 1907.

Runkel, P. J. Cognitive similarity in facilitating communication. *Sociometry*, 1956, *19*, 178–191.

Schachter, S. Deviation, rejection, and communication. *J. abnorm. soc. Psychol.*, 1951, *46*, 190–207.

Scodel, A., Minas, J. S., Ratoosh, P., and Lipetz, M. Some descriptive aspects of two-person, non-zero sum games. *J. conflict Resolut.*, 1959, *3*, 114–119.

Seidman, D., Bensen, S. B., Miller, I., and Meeland, T. Influence of a partner on tolerance for self-administered electric shock. *J. abnorm. soc. Psychol.*, 1957, *54*, 210–212.

Sherif, M. *The psychology of social norms.* New York: Harper, 1936.

Sidowski, J. B., Wyckoff, L. B., and Tabory, L. The influence of reinforcement and punishment in a minimal social situation. *J. abnorm. soc. Psychol.*, 1956, *52*, 115–119.

Singer, R. D. Verbal conditioning and generalization of pro-democratic responses. *J. abnorm. soc. Psychol.*, 1961, *63*, 43–46.

Smith, M. Group judgments in the field of personality traits. *J. exp. Psychol.*, 1931, *14*, 562–565.

Smoke, W., and Zajonc, R. B. On the reliability of group judgments and decisions. In Criswell, J., Solomon, H., and Suppes, P. (Eds.), *Mathematical methods in small group processes.* Stanford, Calif.: Stanford Univ. Press, 1962.

Spence, K. W. *Behavior theory and conditioning.* New Haven, Conn.: Yale Univ. Press, 1956.

Stevenson, H. W., Keen, R., and Knights, R. M. Parents and strangers as reinforcing agents for children's performance. *J. abnorm. soc. Psychol.*, 1963, *67*, 183–186.

Stroop, J. B. Is the judgment of the group better than that of the average member of the group? *J. exp. Psychol.*, 1932, *15*, 550–560.

Suppes, P., and Schlag-Rey, M. Analysis of social conformity in terms of generalized conditioning models. In Criswell, Joan, Solomon, H., and Suppes, P. (Eds.), *Mathematical methods in small group processes.* Stanford, Calif.: Stanford Univ. Press, 1962.

Taffel, C. Anxiety and the conditioning of verbal behavior. *J. abnorm. soc. Psychol.*, 1955, *51*, 496–501.

Thibaut, J. W., and Kelley, H. H. *The social psychology of groups.* New York: Wiley, 1959.

Tinbergen, N. *Curious naturalists.* New York: Basic Books, 1958.

Travis, L. E The effect of a small audience upon eye-hand coordination. *J. abnorm. soc. Psychol.*, 1925, *20*, 142–146.

Triplett, N. The dynamogenic factors in pacemaking and competition. *Amer. J. Psychol.*, 1897, *9*, 507–533.

Turner, E. R. A. Social feeding in birds. *Behavior*, 1964, *24*, 1–46.

Walker, E. L. *Conditioning and instrumental learning.* Belmont, Calif.: Wadsworth, 1966.

Warden, C. J., Fjeld, H. A., and Koch, A. M. Imitative behavior in cebus and rhesus monkeys. *J. genet. Psychol.*, 1940, 56, 311–322.

Warden, C. J., Jenkins, T. N., and Warner, L. H. *Comparative psychology.* New York: Ronald, 1936.

Warren, J. M., and Maroney, R. J. Competitive social interaction between monkeys. *J. soc. Psychol.*, 1958, 48, 223–233.

Weintraub, D. J., and Walker, E. L. *Perception.* Belmont, Calif.: Wadsworth, 1966.

Welty, J. C. Experimental explorations into group behavior of fishes: A study of the influence of the group on individual behavior. *Physiol. Zool.*, 1934, 7, 85–128.

Wenner, A. M. Sound production during the waggle dance of the honey bee. *Animal Beh.*, 1962, 10, 79–95.

Williams, C. D. The elimination of tantrum behavior by extinction procedures. *J. abnorm. soc. Psychol.*, 1959, 59, 269–270.

Wynne-Edwards, V. C. *Animal dispersion in relation to social behavior.* New York: Hafner Publishing Co., 1962.

Zajonc, R. B. The process of cognitive tuning in communication. *J. abnorm. soc. Psychol.*, 1960, 61, 159–168.

—————. A note on group judgments and group size. *Hum. Relat.*, 1962, 15, 177–180.

—————. Social facilitation. *Science*, 1965, 149, 269–274.

Zajonc, R. B., and Burnstein, E. The learning of balanced and unbalanced social structures. *J. Person.*, 1965, 33, 153–163.

Zajonc, R. B., and Smoke, W. Redundancy in task assignments and group performance. *Psychometrika*, 1959, 24, 361–370.

Zander, A., and Medow, H. Individual and group levels of aspiration. *Hum. Relat.*, 1963, 16, 89–105.

SUBJECT INDEX

NAME INDEX